W9-DDA-378

Problems in
Counseling

Problems in Counseling

A CASE STUDY APPROACH

JAMES F. ADAMS

Department of Psychology
Temple University

NEW YORK—THE MACMILLAN COMPANY

With Love
To My Children

Jimmy, Dotty, Bobby

Eighth Printing, 1970

Library of Congress catalog card number: 62–7272

The Macmillan Company
866 Third Avenue, New York, New York 10022
Collier-Macmillan Canada, Ltd., Toronto, Ontario

Printed in the United States of America

Acknowledgments

The author is indebted to Dr. Roy B. Hackman for his helpful suggestions during the preparation of this manuscript. In addition, appreciation should be expressed to the following individuals who have contributed cases for inclusion in this book: Bernard W. Albert, Irwin B. Brenner, Lucille A. Cadden, Charlotte P. Cooper, Vincent Cusatis, Anne Edelmann, Joseph M. Gangemi, Robert G. Gaul, William F. Houser, Florence Howard, Thomas K. Laws, Mary E. Lehman, Irving A. Leshner, Edward G. Lyman, Arnold Medvene, Peggie W. Mullan, Milton U. Oates, Phyllis A. Rogers, Ernest Rubinson, Joseph M. Rucker, and Alexander J. Stavitz. Finally, the author would like to express his appreciation for the constructive comments of his students who have been exposed to the many fragments of this book as it came into being.

Preface

This book of counseling cases has developed from the author's need for such a text in a counselor training program. It was found that the standard sources of case materials were inadequate for several reasons. These cases had generally successful results which tended to create an unrealistic expectancy in the mind of the student; they were limited mainly to school counseling situations and psychiatric settings; and they did not comprehensively cover many of the problems, issues, and techniques with which a counselor should be familiar.

The successful outcome of a case was not a primary consideration for inclusion in this book. Many times, more can be learned from failure than from success. Nor has this casebook been compiled to provide specific answers. It is hoped, however, that the cases will stimulate thinking. The cases are not all complete nor is all the information, that a reader might wish, always given. These cases are not meant to be exhaustive in nature. Rather the intent of the book is to raise problems for thoughtful consideration.

The cases included in this book were chosen for several reasons. First, they were selected because of their situational context. The cases come from elementary school counseling, secondary school counseling, university counseling, private agency counseling, and counseling in private practice. Minimal attention is given to the "run-of-the-mill" case which ordinarily does not present a difficult problem for the counselor.

Secondly, the cases were chosen because of the type of individual or problem to be considered. Problems in educational, vocational, and personal counseling have been included. More specifically, the cases cover counseling in the following areas: wise and unwise vocational choice and educational planning, marriage, incest, delinquency, pregnancy, emotional disturbances, the gifted and retarded, and a number of other areas. The ages of the counselees range from early life to middle age.

The cases were also selected because of the variety of techniques that the counselors utilized, ranging from extreme directivism to non-directivism. The results are sometimes "successful" and sometimes "unsuccessful." Ethical and theoretical problems also entered into the selection of the cases. In the concluding chapter the ethical implications of the cases are considered in detail.

The author believes that counselor trainees should consider the problems, issues, and techniques of counseling both intellectually and emotionally before they meet them experientially. It is further believed that many undesirable outcomes in counseling could have been avoided if the counselor had considered the problem prior to meeting it in practice.

This book has been compiled and written for use in the introductory course in counseling, for advanced counseling courses where the emphasis is on student interaction and participation rather than on the lecture method, and for the practicing counselor. The first person has been used in all of the cases and discussions to emphasize the personal relationship which exists in the counseling process.

Table of Contents

Table of Contents

Table of Contents

Table of Contents

1...
The Role of the Counselor in the Counseling Process

The term *counseling* has been used in so many different contexts to describe such a wide range of activities that one might well ask just what it means. It can be observed that almost every professional group uses the term to refer to at least a part of the services which they offer their clients. Apparently, in many situations, counseling is considered to be nothing more than two individuals talking over a problem which is of major concern to one of the persons involved. This is a most superficial viewpoint; and, to have any real meaning, counseling must be considered as being something more than this. For our immediate purpose let us define counseling as *an interacting relationship between two individuals where one, the counselor, is attempting to help the other, the counselee, to better understand himself in relationship to his present and future problems*. The emphasis in this definition should be upon the term *interacting relationship*. The intensity and depth of this relationship, in conjunction with the nature of the problem of the counselee, are the crucial variables in the counseling process. Tyler (1953, pp. 14–17) * focuses on some of the important elements in counseling when she says:

In the first place, counseling is more than advice giving. . . . Progress comes through thinking that the individual with a problem does for himself rather than through solutions suggested by the counselor. . . . In

* Complete references are listed at the end of the chapter.

the second place, counseling involves more than the solution to an immediate problem. Its function is to produce changes in the individual that will enable him to make wise future decisions as well as to extricate himself from his immediate difficulties. . . . In the third place, counseling concerns itself with attitudes rather than actions. Actions will change as it progresses, but as a result of attitude change. . . . In the fourth place, it is emotional rather than purely intellectual attitudes which are the raw material of the counseling process. Perhaps there is really no such thing as a purely intellectual attitude. . . . Finally, counseling inevitably involves relationships between people, although it may seem to be purely an affair of the one individual who is undergoing it. One of the things hardest for the client to understand is why the thinking he does in the counseling room changes his life more than the thinking he does by himself at home. . . . His relationships with other persons to whom he is bound in various ways take on new meaning. It is because of the importance of this principle that recent writers on the counseling process are stressing relationships rather than techniques, the general structure of the situation rather than the specific rules about what to do and say.

Perhaps, the interacting relationship aspect of counseling can be understood better by using several examples. The student who comes into his counselor's office for information concerning a curriculum choice will receive counseling. However, it is probable that the degree of interaction between this student and his counselor will be rather minimal. Counseling is being done but at a level which requires little involvement on the part of the participants. On the other hand, consider the individual who comes to the counselor with exceptional ability but also with a record of one defeat after another. Here the counselor helps the individual, usually over a protracted period of time, to better understand his own motivations and emotions. The extent to which the counselor aids this individual is likely to depend to a large degree on the relationship which develops during the counseling process between the counselor and the counselee. The depth and intensity of this relationship and the severity of the problem of the counselee may well give an indication of the type of counseling which is being done and the training which is essential in the background of the counselor. Counselors should be well aware of their limitations and sensitive in detecting problems which they are unable to handle.

Counseling and Psychotherapy

There are several questions which are frequently asked: Where does counseling stop and psychotherapy begin? Is there a difference between counseling and psychotherapy? Are the two concepts synonymous? These are not easy questions to answer for there is no sharp line of demarcation between the two concepts. At times counseling is quite distinguishable from psychotherapy; at other times the terms are, indeed, synonymous. Perhaps, the best way to attempt an understanding of the difference between the two terms is by considering them along a continuum of intensity and depth as is shown in the figure below.

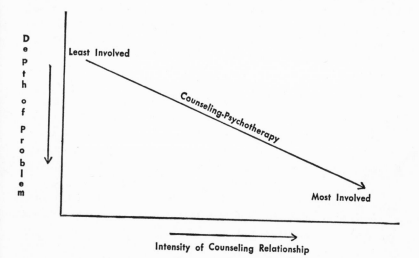

At one end of the continuum, counseling handles problems which are largely cognitive in nature with little affective involvement. These problems are at the surface in consciousness and the relationship between the counselor and the counselee is not an intense one. However, as we go further along the continuum, the problems interact increasingly with the affective or emotional domain. The relationship between the counselor and the counselee, if it is to be beneficial, becomes more intense; and the problems are more personal, deep-seated, and are sometimes at the unconscious level. The whole continuum can be considered counseling, but at some point counseling merges into and becomes synonymous with psychotherapy.

Snyder, in a book entitled *The Psychotherapy Relationship* (1961, p. 2), makes the following observation:

We have also been impressed with how deeply and positively clients have felt toward their therapists, and how much the therapists have reciprocated these feelings. It is evident that therapy is often a major human experience, one of life's high spots, especially for the clients, but also many times for the therapists. We would venture to suggest that many clients have placed their therapists just below their parents in their hierarchy of positive meaningful persons in their lives, and some have undoubtedly placed the therapists above their parents! Rarely do even teachers or other professional persons achieve this need-satisfying status in the lives of another person. Only a person's mate, and often his children, hold positions involving a comparable amount of significance. This is why we use the word therapist, rather than counselor, throughout this book, to describe the person toward whom these intense feelings, sometimes positive and sometimes negative, are developed.

This is a very apt description of the relationship which occurs when counseling and psychotherapy become synonymous, although the present author would disagree that the term counselor must necessarily be deserted for the term therapist when this relationship occurs. There are many adequately trained *counselors* who are engaged in *psychotherapy*. It is true, however, that most school counselors and vocational counselors are not, and for the most part should not be, engaged in psychotherapy. The nature and degree of training for work in this field is quite different from that required for the majority of counseling. Nevertheless, it must be observed that every counselor will, at some time in his career, have cases which will have therapeutic overtones. These are cases where the stated problem falls within the counselor's domain but where he finds, as the case progresses, that the problem is more serious or deep-seated than he may have realized. Experience and ethical considerations (knowledge of one's limitations) dictate that the counselor should proceed with extreme caution in these cases and consider the possibility of referral.

The Role of the Counselor

Counseling may involve making a psychometric assessment of the counselee, the furnishing of information hitherto unknown or unavailable, or being an understanding and empathetic listener. Out of the counseling relationship should come growth and insight for both the counselee and the counselor. The growth for the counselee should better enable him to live more fully; the growth for the counselor should better prepare him for his future helping relationships with other clients.

One of the most basic issues in counseling revolves around the role which the counselor should assume in the counseling process. The fact that this is an issue of considerable concern becomes readily apparent from an examination of the literature in the counseling field. The reason for the difference of opinion as to what role the counselor should assume is caused mainly by disagreement over whether or not the counselee has the basic capability of, and responsibility for, solving his own problems.

If the counselor does not believe that counselees can solve their problems without considerable direct help, then it is apparent that he is likely to be more active in his treatment of an individual counselee and to assume more responsibility for the direction of the counseling sessions.

On the other hand, if one is committed to the belief that the counselee is basically able to solve his own problems and, in the final analysis, is responsible for the conduct of his own life, then the counselor is likely to play a more inactive (perhaps, *less directive* conveys the meaning better) role in the helping relationship. This is, of course, predicated upon the assumption that the counselee is able to initiate his own actions once he is aware of the crucial facts, issues, and motivations which underlie his present impasse.

In the remainder of this chapter, a brief attempt will be made to describe the major roles which counselors have assumed. In a sense these categories are most artificial, for counselors on the whole cannot be typed. Further, many counselors will change roles as a function of the personality and problem of the counselee. The major purpose of the ensuing discussion is to cause the reader to examine his own attitudes toward the roles described. Disagreement over the manner in which the roles are portrayed is desirable if it causes the reader to *think*. Every counselor should examine and reexamine his own counseling procedures. The counselor who is not capable of modification and self-examination has outlived his usefulness.

The Authoritarian Counselor

This counselor is characterized by overtly giving the impression that he has all the answers and by being a self-designated expert in many areas. It is probable that this counselor exists more as a function of his personality than as a result of any personal conviction on his part concerning the role the counselor should assume. His general attitude is that the counselee, by virtue of sitting in front of him, is unable to help himself; and he, by virtue of his wide experience, is obviously better able to solve the counselee's problems. The authoritarian counselor feels quite prepared to tell the counselee exactly what his problem is and what he should do about it.

The subject of authoritarianism in counseling is not an easy subject to discuss as there are times in most counselors' lives when they will take an authoritative action and be quite correct in doing so. When the physical welfare of the client is involved (as in the case of "Please Help Me" in this book), the counselor may have no alternative but to act in an authoritative manner. Furthermore, there are many subtle ways in which a counselor can be authoritative and dominate the counselee. In fact, the counselor may be unaware that his behavior (usually nonverbal) is creating an authoritative impression. Authority may be communicated by mannerisms, intonations of the voice, or through bodily posture and facial expressions. It is possible for a counselor to be authoritative by remaining aloof from the counselee, an untouchable figure, and at the same time react verbally in a nonauthoritative manner. In other words, there are many degrees and ways of being authoritative in the counseling process.

The procedures of the overtly and habitually authoritative counselor are open to question. This counselor uses psychometric data freely and tends to place undue predictive emphasis upon the results. When a counselee is aided by this type of counseling, it might well be asked whether he was helped because of or in spite of the techniques used. This, of course, is a question which a counselor regardless of his orientation might well ask himself. Furthermore, under this orientation it is probable that a counselee will not gain any real understanding of himself; for the decisions which are made for us are not likely to be the ones with which we whole-heartedly agree. Perhaps, even more important is the fact that we will not follow these decisions with the same conviction we would maintain if we made the decisions for ourselves.

Counselor-Centered

While there is no question that the authoritarian type of counseling centers around the counselor, there is a type of counseling which is counselor-centered but is not authoritarian.

As is implied by the term counselor-centered, the focus of the interview or the counseling session is the counselor. There are types of interviews (as distinguished from counseling situations) where this type of orientation is particularly apropos. An example of this is the information type interview which is often the primary function of an employment office in industry. Here the interview is directed toward the receiving and giving of information, not toward the problems of the applicant.

There are times in counseling when the nature of the problem dictates that the situation become counselor-centered. This is not to imply that counseling, in a strict sense, is being done. Consider the case of Buckey in "I've Been Bored." In this case the counselor's pressing problem was to make a decision concerning recommending Buckey to an advanced science program. His interview with Buckey was to inform him of the school's decision. Because of the purpose of the interview, the counselor was quite counselor-centered.

If a counselor adopts this method for a counseling technique, he is likely to believe that the counselee cannot solve his own problems without considerable help. The counselor is very active and expresses his own attitudes freely. He also feels free to evaluate the counselee's expressions and, in general, controls the interaction by leading the discussion. *Talking too much,* one of the cardinal vices of counselors, is particularly likely to become a pitfall for this type of counselor. He also runs into the problem of making premature suggestions and of being too free with his advice. Psychometric data may be used to an excess.

While this may not be the most desirable type of counseling, in all fairness it must be observed that there are some counselors who are able to work with the difficulties inherent in this method and to do an apparently successful job of counseling. It is probable that this method is likely to work best with superficial problems rather than with deep-seated personal problems or involved educational and vocational decisions. Where the primary problem is one of lack of information or misinformation, this procedure may be quite acceptable.

Client-Centered

As the reader is likely to assume, the counselee is the focus in client-centered counseling. The client is encouraged to lead in the counseling discussion and to freely express his attitudes, thoughts, and feelings. The counselor plays a relatively inactive role but is willing to be used as a resource person if the occasion demands it. There is much in common between this type of counselor and the client-centered-non-directive counselor (Wrenn, 1946). The primary difference is that this counselor is more willing to give guidance. That is to say, this counselor believes that there are some situations where the counselee needs help in determining the direction of his life and in the solution of his problems.

The client-centered counselor indicates to the counselee that he is trying to understand, but he does not indicate that he, the counselor, has ultimate truth or the answers to the counselee's problems. The counselor is very careful not to give guidance until he is sure that it is warranted.

The counselor makes use of open-ended questions giving the client every opportunity to express himself. He refrains from interrupting the counselee but does not object if the counselee interrupts him. He believes that the counseling time is the counselee's to use as he wishes. Probing is at a minimum and is done only to clarify what has been said or implied. Facts are important only in relationship to the client's problems. The over-all impression that the counselor attempts to create in the mind of the counselee is that he is interested in the counselee and respects him as an individual.

Psychometric data are used in varying degrees by client-centered counselors. The problem and needs of the counselee dictate the degree of psychometric assessment given (Super, 1950). Frequently, the counselee himself decides whether or not psychological measures will be used. Testing results are interpreted broadly rather than with specific recommendations.

If it is possible, and it usually is, the counselor avoids giving advice and attempts to instill into the client the idea that, in the final analysis, the client must make his own decisions, that he, and he alone, is responsible for himself and his actions. Further, the counselor gives the impression that he has confidence in the counselee's ability to solve his own problems.

The major role of the counselor is to insure that the counselee has a clear comprehension of all the issues which bear upon his problem, that the counselee understands to the best of his ability his own motivations, and, insofar as information is pertinent to the problem, that the counselee has this information available. An example of the client-centered approach in counseling is found in the case entitled "A Successful Failure."

Client-Centered-Non-Directive

The name of Carl Rogers is most closely associated with this approach. In fact, it is the only approach discussed which is closely linked with the name of one individual. Regardless of their orientation, counselors may profit from the study of Rogers' writing (1951; 1957; 1958; 1959).

There are two basic assumptions which help clarify the behavior of the counselor with this orientation. First, the counselor should respect the integrity and personal autonomy of the individual; and second, the individual has the capacity for adaptation and for readjustment, to put it more simply, to solve his own problems.

The contribution of the counselor to the counseling session is largely in the area of attitudes. The counselor maintains an attitude of acceptance and willingness to understand. He tries to see the situation as it appears to the counselee. The counselor is permissive, and the counselee's every expression (short of violence) is permitted. The counselor does not give advice, reason with the counselee, judge the counselee, moralize, or force the counselee to talk. If psychometric data are used at all, their use is minimal (Rogers, 1946).

In his earlier writings Rogers clarified many of the techniques of the counselor. In more recent years he has placed increasing emphasis upon the *relationship* which exists between the counselor and the counselee (e.g., see Rogers' comments in Standal and Corsini, 1959). The major importance of the counselor's attitudes and techniques is in the development of this relationship. It is the relationship which exists between the counselor and counselee which permits the counselee to express himself freely and to bring his feelings out into the open where they can be examined and better understood. The counselor's verbalizings are limited, in the main, to summarizing what the counselee has said and to attempting to distill and clarify the crucial elements or the core of the counselee's expressions. In one sense this may be viewed as lending an element of direction to the counselee; but compared to counselors from outside of this orientation, the method is most non-directive. The case found in this book called "How Far Should I Go?" is an excellent example of client-centered-non-directive counseling.

Eclectic-Counseling

By definition this method of counseling attempts to use any element of the other methods which has a pragmatic value. Counselors within this category can be subdivided into counselors who are eclectic because of practical and theoretical considerations and those who are eclectic because of ignorance.

Many counselors, who have no strong convictions as to the role of the counselor or of the capabilities of the counselee to profit from counseling, claim to be eclectic. This is unfortunate for a loose counseling orientation of this sort frequently implies inadequate training and a lack of conviction concerning the efficacy of one's techniques. Many of these counselors resemble the drowning man who clutches at straws in a vain attempt to save himself. In the past, and to some extent in the present, our public schools have helped to create this counselor. A counseling need is created or discovered and if there is no trained counselor for the position, a person with little or no training is drafted into the post. Sometimes these individuals turn out to be, or become, excellent counselors; more often they do not. In a situation where the demand for counselors is greater than the supply of trained workers, administrators should insist that their untrained counseling personnel remedy their deficiency in training as rapidly as possible.

Harper (1959, p. 156) after an excellent, brief, but clear, description of some thirty-six therapeutic systems, concludes that a careful examination of these systems forces one to a position of eclecticism. His concluding comment applies equally well to counseling and psychotherapy:

Scorning the wrath of the faithful of all systems of psychotherapy, we offer this book as an introduction to therapeutic eclecticism. We are saying, in effect, throughout: look around, reserve judgement for a while and then make it tentative, and experiment with many theories and techniques. Until science brings us definitive answers—if science does—let us try to avoid commitment to a rigid religion of psychotherapy. Let us learn from and constructively employ the arts of many therapies.

When a counselor reaches a position of eclecticism through a careful examination of prevailing theories, techniques, training, and experience, this is one thing. When a counselor calls himself an eclectic because of a theoretical and experiential void, it is questionable whether it is a defensible position.

Is There a Best Counseling Orientation?

There is no conclusive answer to this question. As is true for psychotherapy (Harper, 1959), ultimate truth has not yet been discovered for counseling. The reader might well ask why experimental research has not been conducted to shed light upon this problem. Although the research will not be discussed in this book, the problem has been investigated with, as yet, inconclusive results. Several reasons for this can be considered. First of all, there is a major difficulty in establishing a criterion of success for counseling. Ask yourself, as a reader, how do I know that I have helped my counselee? Did he make some counseling gains of which I was unaware? Was he helped because of me or in spite of me? Should I be satisfied with small changes in the counselee's behavior (Tyler, 1960)? How permanent were the counseling gains? The reader can undoubtedly think of other questions of this type. They all illustrate the difficulty of setting up a criterion of counseling success.

A further problem which plagues research in this area is that there are at least three major variables which contribute to, and sometimes confuse, the counseling process. Defining these variables broadly, they are: the personality of the counselee; the problem of the counselee; and the personality of the counselor. One of the major lessons which counselors can learn from psychology is the lesson on individual differences. Every counselor and every counselee is different from every other counselor and counselee. Nor are there any two problems which are exactly the same. Considering these *facts,* it should become apparent that the techniques used by counselors will vary in effectiveness as a function of these and possibly other variables. In other words, some counselors, as a function of their personalities, will have success with one technique while others will not. As honesty and sincerity are principles which most counselors will agree are desirable, it is probable that if a counselor, after training in a procedural technique, does not feel "comfortable" in using the procedure, he might well consider other methods of operating. What works best for one counselor will not necessarily work best for every counselor. Counselors might also consider whether specific techniques or approaches are the most suitable for certain types of counselees and certain types of problems. Growth in counseling should not be limited to the counselee alone. Counselors need to continually reexamine their techniques, results, and motivations.

None of the foregoing should be construed to imply that research in this area *can not* or *should not* be conducted. It most definitely should be! In spite of the difficulties, research is continuing and becoming more refined (e.g., see Rogers, 1959). However, the final answers are not yet available. If the writer can venture an opinion as to what these answers will be, it is that one of the client-centered approaches will be found to be the most productive in the majority of counseling cases.

The Purpose of This Book

The following chapters contain actual counseling cases. These cases have been chosen to highlight certain problems and issues which face the counselor and with which the counselor should be familiar. The reader should not assume that the procedures used in the cases or the points raised in the discussion sections of the chapters necessarily reflect the viewpoint of the author or any large body of counselors and psychologists. The cases and the discussions have been included in this book to stimulate thought. Further, if the reader is looking for answers and solutions to these problems, he will be disappointed. There are no final answers to many of the problems which arise in counseling. However, it is probable that the counselor will be better prepared for his role if he has intellectually and emotionally considered these problems prior to meeting them experientially in his office.

Finally, there are a number of ethical problems which run through the cases in this book. The concluding chapter, "Ethical Responsibilities of the Counselor in the Counseling Process," discusses the ethical implications of the cases and attempts to lay down some guide lines for the consideration of counselors.

References and Suggested Reading

Arbuckle, D. S. The general counselor: must he be eclectic? *J. consult. Psychol.*, 1951, *15*, 76–78.

Bordin, E. S. *Psychological Counseling.* New York: Appleton-Century-Crofts, Inc., 1955.

Drews, Elizabeth M. (Ed.), *Guidance for the Academically Talented Student.* Wash., D.C.: American Personnel and Guidance Association, 1961.

Harper, R. A. *Psychoanalysis and Psychotherapy—36 Systems.* Englewood Cliffs, N. J.: Prentice-Hall, Inc., 1959.

Rogers, C. R. Psychometric tests and client-centered counseling. *Educ. psychol. Measmt.*, 1946, *6*, 139–144.

——— *Client Centered Therapy.* New York: Houghton Mifflin Co., 1951.

——— The necessary and sufficient conditions of therapeutic personality change. *J. consult. Psychol.*, 1957, *21*, 95–103.

——— The characteristics of a helping relationship. *Personnel guid. J.*, 1958, *37*, 6–16.

——— A theory of therapy, personality, and interpersonal relationships, as developed in the client-centered framework. In S. Koch (Ed.), *Psychology: A study of a Science.* New York: McGraw-Hill Book Co., Inc., 1959.

Snyder, W. J. and Snyder, B. June. *The Psychotherapy Relationship.* New York: Macmillan Co., 1961.

Standal, S. W. and Corsini, R. J. *Critical Incidents in Psychotherapy.* Englewood Cliffs, N. J.: Prentice-Hall, Inc., 1959.

Super, D. E. Testing and using test results in counseling. *Occupations,* 1950, *29,* 95–97.

Tyler, Leona E. *The Work of the Counselor.* New York: Appleton-Century-Crofts, Inc., 1953.

———— Theoretical principles underlying the counseling process. *J. couns. Psychol.,* 1958, *5,* 3–10.

———— Minimum change therapy. *Personnel guid. J.,* 1960, *38,* 475–479.

Williamson, E. G. The fusion of discipline and counseling in the educative process. *Personnel guid. J.,* 1955, *34,* 74–79.

Wrenn, C. G. Client-centered counseling. *Educ. psychol. Measmt.,* 1946, *6,* 439–444.

Wright, E. W. Multiple counseling: why? when? how? *Personnel guid. J.,* 1959, *37,* 551–557.

2...

I Want To Be
An Engineer

Joe is seventeen years old and in the eleventh grade. He came to the counselor's office stating that he was dissatisfied with his grades and wanted to do better.

Joe and his family are relatively new in our community. His father is a salesman for a local manufacturing concern. He has an older brother who is attending one of our state schools and is majoring in engineering. There have been marital problems in Joe's family; his parents have been separated. Although they are now living together, Joe states that another separation is being considered. Apparently, Joe is closer to his mother than to his father. He states that he and his mother used to go to the movies and to other places together. Recently Joe has been dating a Protestant girl of whom his mother does not approve since Joe and his family are Catholics. This seems to have caused some friction between Joe and his mother. While marital problems and Joe's selection of a girl friend are causing some strife in the home, Joe does not seem seriously disturbed over these problems.

Joe attended elementary and junior high school in another city. He enrolled in our school in the tenth grade. The average scholastic ability of the students in our school is somewhat above that of the general population. On a group intelligence test, Joe's classmates obtained a mean I.Q. of 115. Records from Joe's previous school also reveal that Joe was considered to be a model student. However since coming to our school, Joe has been, to some extent, a discipline problem. He has been caught smoking several times and has been in a number of fights.

Joe is in the college preparatory curriculum. His grades for the last two years, with an exception of a "B" in English, have been consistently "C". He has been active in student affairs and seems well liked by his peers. He is a member of several clubs and states that the Photography Club and Speech Club have interested him the most.

The following data, concerning test scores, come from Joe's cumulative record folder.

Test Data	*I.Q.*
Stanford-Binet (administered in the 6th grade)	104
Otis Self Administering Test of Mental Ability (administered in the 9th grade)	110

Iowa Tests of Educational Development (administered in the 10th grade—local norms)

	Percentile
Understanding of Basic Social Concepts	70
Background in Natural Science	41
Correctness in Writing	26
Ability to do Quantitative Thinking	51
Ability to Interpret Reading Materials in Social Studies	55
Ability to Interpret Reading Materials in Natural Sciences	49
Ability to Interpret Literary Materials	40
General Vocabulary	46
Use of Sources of Information	19

Kuder Preference Record (administered in the 11th grade, Form CH, National Norms)

	Percentile		*Percentile*
Outdoor	45	Artistic	44
Mechanical	80	Literary	67
Computational	16	Musical	13
Scientific	76	Social Service	33
Persuasive	95	Clerical	9

Strong Vocational Interest Blank For Men (administered in the 11th grade, "B" and "A" interest areas only)

Engineer   Sales Manager   Personnel Director   Public Administrator

California Test of Personality (administered in the 11th grade). Although he is slightly below average in Family Relations and School Relations, Joe's profile on the California Test reveals no areas of severe maladjustment.

Counseling Sessions

As Joe had stated that he was concerned about his marks, we talked about this problem. It became apparent that Joe's study habits were acceptable; and, if anything, the amount of time he devoted to his studies was above average. During the course of our conversation, Joe revealed that his concern was really not with his marks but rather with the possibility of being accepted into a college engineering program. I asked Joe why he wanted to be an engineer. His reply was a little vague and seemed to center around the fact that his brother was finishing his senior year in college in an engineering program, that engineers made a lot of money, and that our country had to keep up with Russia. I asked Joe if he would like to have some information concerning the training of engineers and the types of positions which engineers took upon graduation from college. Then I pulled several pamphlets from our occupational file and gave them to Joe. We made another appointment for the following day.

The next day Joe came into the office and laid the engineering pamphlets on my desk. "You know," he said, "engineers do everything I don't like to do." He went on to say that mathematics was his most difficult course and that, even if he could get through his training, he wouldn't be too interested in being an engineer. I asked him why he had thought he wanted to be an engineer. "I guess it was because my brother was so interested in engineering," he replied.

At this point I asked him if he would be interested in looking at some of his interest inventory scores. We discussed them, at some length, with respect to broad areas of occupations where these interests might be utilized. Finally Joe asked, "Mr. ——, do you think I'm smart enough to go to college?" He went on to point out that he knew he wasn't the most brilliant person in the world but that he did want to go on with his education. I told Joe that while intelligence was important for success in college, there were other things equally as important. "For example, your *wanting* to go to college is very important if this means that you would be willing to study very hard." I went on to talk a little about the difference in the admission standards of various colleges. I pointed out to Joe that, while his ability might be a little below the average for some colleges, there were individuals of his ability level going to these schools. Some of them would graduate and some would not. The difference between these two groups was probably a result of how much they wanted a college education.

Joe and I had one last meeting together. In this session Joe brought up the problem of his uncertainty concerning what he wanted to be. He knew that he wanted to go to college, but he didn't know what he wanted to major in. I pointed out to Joe that while this was a real problem, it was also a common one for high school students and college students. I added that most colleges recognized this and therefore had made provisions for indecision. The first two years in college is a period when students take courses which are broad in nature; thus the student has an opportunity to find an area of interest. I showed Joe the curriculum from several catalogues of colleges that I thought he might wish to attend. As Joe seemed satisfied and did not request another interview, this was our last session.

Discussion

In talking with students, every counselor makes certain decisions concerning problem areas. Other counselors might well ask why I didn't talk with Joe about his home relationships or his disciplinary problems in school. Perhaps these areas could have been investigated so that Joe would have profited from the experience. I did not bring up these areas for several reasons. First of all, while Joe did have problems in his home, he seemed to be handling them well, and they were not disturbing him to any great extent. I think a school counselor should avoid getting into this area whenever possible. If Joe had wished to talk about his home situation, I would have listened but would not have given any advice. With respect to the school discipline problem, it seems to me that much of what is labeled into this area is a normal result of maturation in the student. In other words I did not see this as a problem area, and consequently I did not bring it up in my sessions with Joe. His basic problem, as I saw it, was an unwise vocational choice based on insufficient information. I attempted to remedy this situation but did not insist that Joe change his vocational choice to another field. I did not feel that Joe was ready to make a vocational decision. I think counselors, parents, and adults are all too eager to force vocational decisions on adolescents before they are capable of making such decisions. It seems to me that, in this area, the major duty of the counselor is frequently to present accurate and broadly oriented occupational information, to help the individual know himself, and to trust that, when a decision is finally made, the individual will have the data he needs to make a wise decision.

3...
A Successful Failure

Barry came into my office and said, "Dr. ——, I'd like to talk with you about becoming a physician." This was hardly a startling statement; but, considered in the context of Barry's life, it was a most interesting one.

A few years before Barry had come to our college from the army. He had majored in physical education, had been an outstanding athlete and a student leader. Now he was a successful football coach in a small high school. His grades in college had not been brilliant, but they had been acceptable. His college entrance examinations revealed that he had average intellectual ability.

I invited Barry to sit down and then went on to ask him what had caused his interest in medicine. He told me that he had married a nurse and was becoming increasingly more fascinated with the medical field. He had talked with a number of physicians concerning their work, spent several days accompanying them on their rounds, watched them operate in surgery, and now felt that he understood quite well the duties of the profession. I asked him if the doctors had also pointed out some of the unattractive sides to their work and training. He answered that he had questioned them about this and that he thought they had been quite honest in their answers. As we talked further, it became apparent that Barry had thoroughly investigated the medical area.

Barry had also talked with the premedical advisor at our college. They had discussed the course work he would have to make up and the standards he would have to maintain in order to be accepted for admission to medical school. They had agreed that it might be well for Barry to come and talk with me before a final decision was made.

I asked Barry what he thought I could contribute. He answered that he had some doubts as to his intellectual ability and wondered if I would give him an individual intelligence test. "Also," he said, "I would like to have your advice on this decision as it is a very important one." I smiled and remarked that, having had several psychology courses from me, he should remember I did not give advice; however, I would be more than willing to help him make a decision.

We went on to talk of the financial problems that Barry would face. He had considered this problem realistically and had decided that while finances would be "tight," they could be worked out. I asked Barry how he liked his teaching and coaching and found that he enjoyed both and had had winning teams over the last two years. We concluded the interview by scheduling a testing session and also planned for one other counseling session.

The Concluding Interview

Barry came into my office for the last interview. He did not appear anxious but was his usual self-confident self. Perhaps I should also add that, in my contacts with Barry over several years, I had concluded he was one of the most delightfully well-adjusted individuals I had ever known.

"Well, Dr.——," he asked, "how did I do on that intelligence test?" I told him that the Wechsler tended to substantiate the group testing results and that his measured intellectual ability was within the average range (Full Scale I.Q. of 106; both the verbal and performance I.Q. were quite similar). "I rather expected as much," he commented. "How does this compare with the measured ability of physicians?" I replied that undoubtedly there were a few physicians with this level of intellectual ability; however, they were very few indeed. This brought up the topic of medical school standards and, perhaps a subject of equal importance, the role that motivation plays in one's success. I noted that one of the reasons for the imperfect predictive ability of our measuring instruments is that we have not yet devised an adequate measure of motivation.

Barry looked at me directly and asked, "Dr. ——, you don't think that I will be successful if I pursue a medical education, do you?"

"Barry," I replied, "I can't say that you won't be successful if you proceed with your plans. However, from the viewpoint of my past experience and from what we know about success in the medical profession, the probability is that you will not be successful. But, the final decision is yours to make. You may be the exception that disproves the rule. I believe that you have a good grasp of all the factors which should enter into your decision and that whatever your decision is, it will be the right one."

Barry sat quietly for a few moments. He then looked at me and said, "Dr. ——, I want to be a doctor more than anything else in this world. If I don't try, I know I will always wish I had. I fully understand what you have said to me and realize that it will be an uphill struggle. But I *am* going to try." I shook hands with him and assured him that if he wished to talk with me at a later date I would be happy to see him.

Shortly after this counseling session, I resigned to accept a position at another university. I did not hear from Barry again and several years passed before I was able to ascertain the outcome of the case. I had returned to the area on business and contacted Barry's premedical advisor. He informed me that he had never seen a student with more motivation. Barry had spent long hours in the science laboratories, but he had been unable to master the basic science courses which were prerequisite to the medical program. He went on to say that Barry was now back in coaching, was successful, and apparently was a very happy individual.

Discussion

I believe this case is of interest for several reasons. First of all, I was convinced that of the many counselees who have come into my office, Barry had the clearest grasp of the problems which faced him. I had the feeling, at all times, that his thinking was extremely rational and clear. At least it was as rational as being human permits one to be. Secondly, contrary to Barry's belief that if I were to give advice I would suggest that he should not try the premedical program, I thought he made the right decision. That is to say, if I had had to make his decision for him, I would have made exactly the same one that he did and for precisely the same reason. I think that failure, even though predictable in advance, is sometimes the desirable alternative. I believe that Barry was correct in his thinking that he *must attempt* to win the goal he desired; that otherwise he would go through life wishing he had. I wish I could talk with Barry today and ask him what difference this failure has made in his life. I would venture to say that he is happier because of it. It was indeed a successful failure.

4...

I've Been Bored

Buckey is a very bright boy of fourteen. He has a Binet I.Q. of 150. Buckey is also a trouble-maker of the first order and his teachers' comments from the first grade on have been consistently negative. His school marks have been just about average, mostly "C's" with a few "B's" and an occasional "A." Buckey has been in our junior high school for about two and a half years. He has been suspended on several occasions for fighting and for acquiring too many detentions. He seems to take these suspensions lightly. The principal has frequently been in touch with Buckey's parents by letter and by telephone.

There seems to be no love lost between Buckey and any teacher in the junior high school. Most of the teachers consider his classroom behavior poor. In fact, because of his past record, they expect him to become a serious problem sooner or later. All of his teachers, especially those who teach mathematics and science, seem to recognize Buckey's potential ability. However, most of the time they cannot get enough work out of him to warrant a good grade. Buckey has a keen interest in science and mathematics but he feels that his teachers may be a little lacking in knowledge in these areas. As he told the principal, "No teacher here has had any advanced physics; they don't understand me."

Buckey closely identifies with his 22-year-old brother who is currently working on his Ph.D. in mathematics. Buckey's brother has told him that school grades are not important and that with his ability he will be able to get into just about any college he desires to enter.

Recently, when Buckey's behavior was especially poor, the principal telephoned his home. His mother listened while the principal

24

explained the problem and the school's position; then she said, "I'd like you to talk to my son, John." John, Buckey's older brother, wanted to know what the trouble was. He said that he could see nothing wrong with his brother being constantly late to classes. John also said that, while he was not Buckey's guardian, they discussed things at home in a communal fashion and that Buckey talked to him more than he did to his parents. The principal expressed the view that John's attitude seemed to be argumentative and that he would not discuss the situation further with him. He added that if Buckey's mother had anything further to say, then John should return the phone to her. John continued to talk with no response from the principal who finally terminated the conversation by hanging up the phone.

Buckey's parents report that his behavior at home is fine and that they feel the school is picking on him.

Buckey is very much interested in being enrolled next year in the advanced science and mathematics course given in high school. In order for a student to be admitted to the advanced program, which is limited to twenty-five exceptional boys and girls, he must have the recommendation of his principal and guidance counselor. In this particular instance, the decision to recommend or not to recommend rests entirely in my hands for reasons which are not pertinent to this case. To clarify the problem in my own mind, I have asked our principal and Buckey's science and mathematics teachers to submit to me in writing their opinion as to whether or not Buckey should be recommended for this program. Their comments are as follows:

The principal:

I am definitely against recommending Buckey. He has not been a good student here in junior high, and I do not see how he could change enough to get along in the advanced program. They will not tolerate a person whose behavior continually disrupts classroom activities and regular school routine. Buckey is what I would call a real "mess."

The science teacher:

Buckey most certainly has not been a model student, but he has done fairly good work in science. He has a relatively thorough knowledge of biology and elementary physics and chemistry. I know he is intelligent. Therefore, in spite of his poor behavior, I suggest that Buckey be recommended for the advanced program.

The algebra teacher:

> Buckey is a "know-it-all" type of student who has a higher opinion of himself than he deserves to have. He could be a good math student if he changed some of his attitudes. He thinks he knows more about math than I do. I feel that a place in the advanced program could probably be more advantageously used if given to someone else. I strongly suggest that Buckey not be recommended for the program.

Buckey knows it will be difficult for him to get a recommendation from his junior high school. He has suddenly become concerned about this and often stops to talk with his science and mathematics teachers, hoping to convince them that he should be allowed to enter the science program. Indirectly he is also trying to convince them that he has seen the error of his ways. After fully considering the matter, I made an appointment with Buckey. He knew he would receive the final decision at this time.

The Concluding Session

When Buckey came into my office, he was polite and understandably anxious. I opened the interview by asking him why he thought he should be recommended for the science program. He replied, "I'm intelligent enough to handle the accelerated program. The work in this school has been too easy. I don't think the teachers, at least most of them, have a very good background in the sciences. I think that if I had been challenged by my teachers, my work would have been better. I would have been more interested. Up to this year I have been bored in most of my classes. This year algebra isn't too bad."

I asked Buckey if he realized why the principal and some of the teachers might be reluctant to recommend him. He seemed to have no difficulty in understanding their reluctance. We discussed his past attitude, behavior, and work habits. Buckey recognized, intellectually at least, his need for improvement in these areas. He said that he was certain that there would be progress all along the line if he were enrolled in the advanced science and mathematics course.

I told Buckey, "Even though I have several doubts, I am going to recommend you for this program. I hope that you do not disappoint either yourself or me."

My reasons for making the decision to recommend Buckey were as follows:

1. He is very bright.
2. He has a keen interest in the sciences.
3. He apparently has an aptitude for science and mathematics.
4. I felt that the reasons which Buckey gave for his lack of success in the junior high school were fairly sound. That is, if he were placed in a fast group with more advanced subject matter, he would give a good account of himself and enjoy school more than he does at the present time.

Discussion

It seems to me that there are at least three problems in this case which I shall discuss separately. First of all, it is apparent that up to this point counseling with Buckey can best be described as having been a glaring failure. How do you help a student whose parents do not feel that he needs help? Even more pertinent, how do you help a student change his behavior when he feels that it is perfectly acceptable? I am of the opinion that nothing can be done in a situation such as this.

Secondly, I believe that Buckey may have hit upon some truth when he claims that his school environment was not stimulating. Apparently he put some of his teachers on the defensive. Be that as it may, how can a counselor help in this area? Or, can he?

Lastly, although I believe I was correct in deciding to recommend Buckey for the science program, I can understand how others might not agree with me. Would more of a beneficial nature have been accomplished for Buckey if he had not been recommended? In other words if Buckey had not been recommended, would this major catastrophe have taught him a needed lesson?

5...

He Had
What It Takes

Lew was referred to me by his eighth grade English teacher who had made out the following referral report:

Lew's attitude in class is mainly one of nonchalance and disinterest. He works individually only under constant supervision. Lew has submitted none of the three major assignments. He is far behind his classmates in his other work as well. At this date Lew's grade is "D". In spelling he has an "F". His work in literature is of "A" quality. He does especially well in context testing. I do not believe that he has read the stories but instead has relied upon the class discussion for his knowledge. In a library session, the librarian gave Lew a "B". Supposedly he had to memorize the Dewey Classification System to earn such a mark. Lew completely puzzles me. His home life may be a factor. I believe that he is above average in intelligence but does not seem to understand that it is impossible to study only that which appeals to him. Lew talked to me today to ask if he was failing. I told him that he was not but attempted to explain how poorly he was doing. Perhaps what Lew needs is to fail. This might do more than pushing, threatening, or lecturing him. Lew is not an overt discipline problem. Any disturbance he causes is by not paying attention or causing me to break into my procedures in an attempt to lure him back to reality.

Other reports from Lew's math, science, and history teachers indicated that Lew had the ability to do better than average work but because of his uninterested attitude, he was just passing.

After reading the various reports concerning Lew, I checked his school record which was quite revealing. Within a period of seven years, Lew had attended elementary schools in Nevada, California, and Georgia. His father had been an outstanding engineer who had designed and built bridges and dams for the U.S. Government. While living in Georgia, Lew had maintained an "A" average in the fifth, the sixth, and seventh grades. In fact, because of Lew's "A" average and high I.Q. of over 120, plans had been made for him to skip the eighth grade. These plans had been forgotten because of a highway accident in which his father had been killed. After this accident, Lew and his mother had moved to our community.

I checked into Lew's background as thoroughly as I could before I requested him to come in and see me during his study period. He seemed cheerful but cautious and talked only when spoken to. I felt that he expected me to give him a lecture about his grades. When he realized that the session was not to follow his expectations, he began to look around the room. He noticed two model bridges on my desk and his expression changed completely. He asked, "Who made them?" When I replied that I did, he looked me straight in the eye for the first time. We discussed various types of bridges, and he began to tell me about a project he had begun recently. He had spent two days building a dam in the stream behind his home so that he might find out if his homemade waterwheel would turn fast enough to generate electrical power. For ten or fifteen minutes we discussed various uses of homemade waterwheels. I sketched a small waterwheel and illustrated how certain gears and other attachments might be used to do different jobs. I ended the demonstration by showing how I had rigged up an attachment to a waterwheel to crack nuts and acorns at our summer home in the mountains. Following this demonstration, Lew commented, "You know, I really enjoy talking to people who have what it takes." Being a little surprised at his comment, I asked him to explain what he meant. Lew's explanation ran as follows:

"You've got what it takes," was my Dad's favorite expression. He used to deal with many people. If he liked them and felt they did a good job, he would say, "You know, you've got what it takes." He certainly had what it takes. If he were here and did not like the situation, he'd just see that things would change. He'd make everything just as he wanted it. My Mom and I miss him a great deal. He always knew all the answers. It seems as though no one in this place can understand the importance of having what it takes.

I told Lew that his father must have been a fine man. Then I asked him, "How does a person get what it takes?" Just then the bell rang, I thanked Lew for coming in and asked if he would like to return the next day during his activity period. He agreed to come in and seemed pleased over the prospect of another meeting. I told him to give my last question some thought, shook his hand, and said goodby.

The following day Lew arrived in my office just as I opened the door. He seemed to be anxious to get the session under way. As soon as we sat down, Lew began to explain what "having what it takes" meant to him. He felt that such a person was liked and respected because of his achievement and his understanding of others. I then asked him what achievement was and how did people achieve something. He believed that achievement occurred when one advanced in his field or with his work. He felt that the only way to achieve something was to work hard. I indicated to Lew that I agreed with his definition and proceeded to use these definitions to stimulate his evaluation of himself.

A Productive Insight

Lew seemed to begin to realize that a climax was near, and his speech slowed down. Feeling that part of the reason for his slower response was being unsure of what he wanted to say, I began to question him more directly. I asked Lew if he felt that his achievement in school was good. He seemed stunned for a moment and then replied that he thought it was poor. He said that he felt his teachers had no appeal and were not very understanding. I asked him if he felt that he had been sincere in evaluating them. Finally, after some hesitation, he agreed that he had not. I asked him if he worked hard and tried to do his best in school. Again he replied that his teachers did not appeal to him enough to demand full effort on his part. He stated, "They just don't have what it takes." There was a pause, and then Lew said, "I guess I expected them to help me like Dad helped me." He then began to cry. After a few minutes he composed himself, and I asked him if he would like to proceed. He stated that he had a lot to think about, and he would rather come in again in a day or two. I agreed and made an appointment to meet Lew during the middle of the next week.

Lew was a changed person at our next session. He stated that he understood what he had been doing and that he was going to change. I asked Lew if he felt that his problem had been solved. He said that it had, and we began to discuss his reasoning. Lew stated that he now knew he had been kidding himself about his relationship with his teachers. He felt that his grief over the loss of his father would heal in time but that he had never noticed the rut he was in until our sessions had begun. He thanked me for helping him. I stated that he was welcome to come back to my office at any time he wished.

Discussion

Following each of the three counseling sessions, many questions passed through my mind. At the end of the first session, I wondered if I had completely gained the boy's confidence. I believe that I was fortunate in having had some interests similar to Lew's and that these mutual interests broke the initial ice. I try to keep a number of "attention-getters," which could be topics of conversation for my counselees, placed around the room. I have found these objects to be quite helpful.

After the second session I wondered if I had pushed the issue too hard. At the time I felt that Lew had the ability to gain a sudden insight into his problem. I purposefully did not sympathize with him concerning the loss of his father for I felt that this would have been useless. What he needed was to realize that he was not living up to the standards which he held for both himself and others. I agreed with Lew when he indicated that he wished to think about this by himself rather than discuss it further, because it seemed to me that he had made the initial breakthrough. I did, however, ask myself whether Lew's unwillingness to continue the discussion was an attempt, on his part, to escape from a painful situation which I had created.

I thought that the last session was productive in that it gave Lew the opportunity to verbalize his mistakes and to express a new found understanding of himself. I believe that Lew has solved his problems and will grow into a most productive adult. In conclusion I would like to add that Lew is not a typical case in counseling. He had reached the point in his thinking where he was ready for insightful thinking. Unfortunately, many of a counselor's cases will not be as easy to resolve as this one was.

6...
I Failed as a Counselor

Joan was a seventeen-year-old high school senior. As a teacher-counselor I became aware of her about two and one half years ago, shortly after she had entered our three-year senior high school.

As is true in many schools, our school has a detention hall which meets at the close of each school day. Each teacher is assigned detention duty about once every six weeks. Toward the close of Joan's first semester in high school, I became aware of the fact that Joan was in detention hall practically every time I met with the group. As I began to observe her, it became readily apparent that she had a problem. From the guidance files came anecdotal evidence which confirmed my observations. For example, one of Joan's teachers wrote as follows:

Joan's attitude is negative! Although she usually has a fresh-scrubbed appearance and is able to do better than average work when she wants to, she very often acts contrary to what one would expect. At times she comes to class wearing pin-curls and expects to be excused to the girl's room to take down her hair; thus, half a period is wasted. When she returns, she is unaware of the activity in progress. She just sits and wastes time during the second half of the period, not even attempting to open a book unless nagged to do so. She refuses to conform and perform in the accepted classroom manner. She violates basic classroom rules. She often chews gum, publicly demands to have her seat changed to the rear of the room, often deliberately changes seats without permission, constantly attempts to write personal notes and do everything and anything that the class is not doing at the moment. At times she talks excessively, at other times she is morbidly quiet, sulks, etc.

32

To summarize the comments of Joan's teachers, she did not go along with the decisions made by either the teachers or the class. She was quarrelsome and became angry very easily. She appeared to be resentful, defiant, and sullen. She refused to do her assignments or to contribute in any meaningful way to the class. On the positive side, she did respond to individual, non-academic activity. She volunteered to act as a messenger, to distribute classroom materials, and to assist in routine chores. Her academic achievement, however, was poor in all of her courses.

In talking with Joan's mother, I couldn't find that Joan's home life was any different than hundreds of other homes. Her parents were lax in applying discipline and preferred to "talk" with Joan rather than to administer punishment in more drastic forms. Joan's parents were worried about her behavior. Her mother had worked most of her married life but recently stopped because of her concern for her daughter. Joan's father is a civil service employee and provides for his family in an acceptable, if not luxurious, manner.

Joan was asked to come to my office. While she was polite, my impression was that she did not trust me, and no matter how hard I tried I could not seem to instill confidence in her. We talked about her school work and her attitude in class and she readily admitted that she didn't care whether or not she received credit for her classes. She didn't feel that her teachers understood her; she knew that her actions were unacceptable, but she just didn't care. I did not pressure Joan, but I listened to her comments and tried to understand her. When I asked her what she thought was the reason for her behavior, she replied that she felt that she was a product of her environment. "Most of the time I get what I ask for. I have my own way a lot. I really shouldn't be allowed to have my own way at home because then I want my own way when I am around my friends at school. And when I can't have my own way, I rebel and get mad."

Over several years I talked with Joan from time to time and continued to try to win her confidence. She spoke freely of her social activities. She dated freely and apparently was popular. Her mother reported that Joan orders her friends around a great deal with apparently no ill effects. Joan implied to me that she, as many of her girl friends, had sexual contact with some of her boy friends. Occasionally she spoke of her friends disparagingly and intimated that she would like to stop associating with them.

I had Joan in my history class in her junior year in high school. Her behavior had not changed. She did barely passing work. Her assignments were not done or were handed in late; in general her behavior was most unsatisfactory. It was a difficult time, for my dual roles as a teacher and as a counselor were in continual conflict. As a teacher, I could not accept Joan's behavior; as a counselor I still wanted to gain her confidence and to try to help her.

As a result of Joan's constant violations of the school attendance law, near the close of her junior year, she and her parents were referred to the Juvenile Court. The case was just about to be dismissed with the imposition of a fine on the parents when, in a side conversation with her mother, Joan became loud and sarcastic. The Judge who was considering her case became angry at her behavior and immediately sentenced her to one month in the County Detention Home.

Joan returned home a changed person. At least she seemed outwardly changed. Her parents were understandably very concerned and initiated psychiatric treatment. However, this treatment was terminated after two sessions. During Joan's senior year, her behavior has been, by school standards, much more acceptable. She is quiet, slightly withdrawn, and in general neutral in her attitudes. Although she is still achieving below her ability, she is passing most of her required subjects and is likely to graduate in about four weeks.

I would predict that upon graduation Joan will find a clerical job of some sort, work for a limited period of time, and then will probably get married. Most definitely she has not changed inwardly; she still does not understand herself and has not found a place for herself either emotionally or socially. In short, I feel that her school experience has not been a profitable one.

Discussion

I will be quite frank. As a counselor, I have failed miserably with this girl. Why have I failed? I believe the answer to this can be found in the multiplicity of roles which I have had to assume. Joan saw me as Mr. ——, the detention hall supervisor; Mr. ——, the history teacher; and therefore *not* as Mr. ——, her counselor. Joan needed someone to whom she could talk; someone who was completely divorced from her problems. I was not. No matter how sincere I was in attempting to understand Joan and in gaining her confidence, it was an impossible task. I believe that Joan has caused me to seriously doubt that a counselor can function as a counselor and, at the same time, assume the other duties which I have described. Most certainly this would be true with many individuals. I wonder if we should not give further consideration as to the advisability of being both a teacher and a counselor at the same time. I also wonder if there was some way in which I could have helped Joan. I wish I knew the answer to these questions.

7...
Nobody
Understands Me

Ellen was an alert, eighth-grade girl. Her parents had come to me expressing concern over her temper outbursts, her sudden lack of interest in school, and her belligerent attitude toward her mother. They thought that there was more to her behavior than could be explained by normal adolescent development. Her parents asked if I would attempt to discover what was causing Ellen's problem. I replied that I would be very happy to talk with Ellen and then explained to them what counseling would entail. If gains were made, they would see these as a change in Ellen's behavior. I added that, in order to hold Ellen's confidence, I would not be able to report to them directly unless I had her permission. They agreed to cooperate in any way that they could.

Counseling

In the first counseling session, Ellen and I got to know each other. I asked her about her school work and any plans she might have after completing school. When asked about her plans after high school, she replied, "I want to go to college as far away from home as possible." I reflected her feeling, and she said, "Yes, I wish I could go now. I want to return home as little as possible and live my own life." I pointed out to her that many teen-agers felt this way.

During the next session Ellen talked freely about her home problems. She was able to discuss them intelligently and seemed to verbalize quite freely. She appeared relaxed and acted happy to have someone listen to her. Upon request she amplified and clarified her statements. Her comments went as follows:

I can talk to my father. He understands me better. But I even said something to hurt him this week. (Her parents had previously reported to me that at the end of a particularly stormy session, Ellen had shouted to both of them, "I hate you!") I never, never want to get married. I don't want to be burdened with children. My mother doesn't like to cook. She'll do anything to take short cuts and get out of the kitchen. My mother doesn't bother to take time for fixing meals. We often have the same old thing. I've had so much chicken chow mein from the delicatessen that I can't stand the stuff. She wouldn't make french fries herself—too much bother. They're always frozen. She freezes everything so food won't be so much trouble. My sister is younger and she gets most of the breaks. My sister and I aren't allowed to touch each other when we fight, so we fight with words a lot. When I want to buy something, my mother says we don't have the money. But when she wants something she gets it. I wish I could do things for myself. When I work in the kitchen, I don't like someone else standing over me. I wish my mother would see my side of it sometimes. When we argue, it always ends her way. She has to win. I want to leave home just as soon as I can and not come back. After college, I want a career and want to travel.

By this time I was convinced that Ellen was going through an understandable phase of growing up. Understandable, that is, by the very frequency of its occurrence. Girls of this age tend to isolate themselves from others when they have difficulties; and consequently they believe that no one else has had the same experience.

I said, "Ellen, I would like to read to you a list of problems which another girl of your age wrote down. Would you like to hear them?" Ellen nodded in the affirmative, and I read the following list which had been written by a thirteen-year-old girl and was entitled: "Proper Etiquette for Mothers' Relationships with Their Daughters (Teen Age)":

1. Never suggest that they are tired, cranky, hot, or cold. Let them tell you of their discomfort themselves.

2. Never interrupt them when they are telling stories, etc., no matter how important you think it is unless it is simply a *dire necessity*. Do something else until the tale is finished.

3. Show *absolutely no* partiality to another brother or sister, especially in the matter of running errands. Have it understood that they are taking turns.

4. No matter how angry or impatient, or surprised you are, never scream, cry, yell, or talk loudly. They'll admire it if you keep a cool, matter-of-fact, businesslike manner. It will always do more for results anyway than shouting when nervous. Keep your voice in control.

5. Don't have it understood as a hard and fast rule, but once in awhile plan surprises for your daughter, to remind her that you are constantly thinking of her pleasures, but not hers only. Plan a party, buy a new dress, plan a good movie and have her take a girl friend occasionally.

6. *Don't* force her confidence, and when she does tell you surprising things, don't make a side show out of it. Just answer in a matter-of-fact tone and she'll tell you more. They don't like emotional outbursts.

7. It's a good idea to have something nice for her handy, so when she's cross, you just give it to her quietly, and she'll be so ashamed she'll treat you ten times better. It works better than scolding and sometimes pleadings. Always have an even tone of voice. Don't get emotional and excited. She's liable to be more comrady if you are like this, because she's used to that kind of disposition in her other friends.

8. Praise her for good work as often as it is rightly due. Don't turn her head though.

9. Above all things, don't keep referring to "that awful teen age." It makes them self conscious and they won't confide in you so much for fear you'll say that. Even though you and your friends say it only in fun, it will usually do more harm than good.

10. Don't contradict your daughter sharply to her face just for something to say. A good example is when your daughter says, "I need a new basketball. My other one is shot to pieces." And you say, "Oh, I don't think it is!" (When you really haven't even looked at it!) If you're trying to save money, tell her so, don't contradict like you know all about it when you don't.

11. Try to be understanding. When your daughter gets hysterical over a detail, don't say, "Oh you'll be all right soon." To her, it is a big matter, and you ought to treat it as such. Try to reason it out together and give her your comfort and attention. She will appreciate it more than you know!

12. Don't govern her too hard; she likes freedom and plenty of it. Let her choose what dress she'll wear, continually, unless it is really absurd. She likes to fly her own wings. Let her make decisions occa-

sionally. Take her into the family secrets, and she'll feel important. She won't tell if you caution her not to. It's really good experience in keeping secrets, and makes her feel you can trust her.

13. When your daughter's complexion is bad, try to make helpful suggestions, but *don't keep referring to this ailment very often.* It will be a source of friction.

14. When your daughter's "monthly" comes along, it isn't necessary to talk about it *at all* unless she brings the subject up herself. Of course, warn her that you should be notified at once if she has any difficulties.

15. When discussing a serious question (such as morals) with your daughter—no matter how badly you feel she is wrong, *do not get heavy* over your point. Saying "you break my heart" and crying is very annoying no matter how much she loves you.

16. *Be Young in actions! Be Gay around her!* Act young and you'll always be pals.

17. *Motto to Follow:* "Being tired is suicide to happy family relations." Take a day off if you feel this way—go and do something exciting and rest. Never say, "I'm so tired!", if you want to appear young.

18. When your daughter goes on a short trip (weekend) welcome her back with cheer and a "special supper" for her. Make her feel that you're especially happy to have her back. See that you and the family are dressed up and neat.

19. Be *very careful* about imposing yourself on your daughter's plans. She likes to feel a certain amount of independence! For instance, if she plans on a picnic with friends, don't invite yourself along. Be backward in this respect. If she really wants you, she'll invite you; of course in this way you may feel free to go.

20. *A very important fact* to bear in mind is that a girl doesn't relish her mother's talking of her "personal" intimate matters within her father's hearing when she is around. If it must be done, for *goodness sake* don't let her know about it. *This is extremely important!*

As I read, Ellen nodded her head obviously identifying with the list. When I had completed the list, she said, "I have the same problems except for two of them. Isn't that something?"

During our next counseling session, I felt that Ellen had gained some insight when she said that if she stopped to think before she spoke at home she might understand that her mother also had problems. At this point I asked, "Ellen, even though you don't understand your parents sometimes, do you feel that underneath all the troubles they really love you and want the good things in life for you?" She readily agreed with this, and I went on to ask, "I wonder if it is possible for them to welcome any suggestions you may have for improving your relationships with them?"

Ellen responded, "I can't talk with my mother because she gets excited and hurt. My father is O.K., but he always backs her up." I then asked Ellen if she would consider my talking with her parents in an attempt to get them to understand what she had told me. Ellen replied without hesitation that she thought that if someone from outside the family would explain things it "might help."

Feeling that Ellen had progressed as far in counseling as she needed to, I asked her parents to come in for a concluding session. I discussed with them the general content of Ellen's feelings and showed them the problem list with which Ellen had identified so closely. I pointed out to them the difficulty of understanding those who are the closest to us. I also told them that their "wanting to understand" their daughter indicated to me that they could understand her and that talking quietly with her when there were problems to be discussed would further a mutual understanding. Ellen's parents seemed to accept what I said, and so we concluded the session.

About a month later, I accidentally saw Ellen and stopped her to ask how things were going at home. She smiled and replied, "Things are a lot different."

Discussion

I have discussed this case because of the familiar aspect of the problem involved. Many adolescents go through a period when they feel that they are misunderstood and that no one has ever experienced the problems they are experiencing. They seldom realize that their parents are human and also have problems and that because of their love for their children, they are so emotionally involved that they can make mistakes in their very desire to understand them. I have found this "problem list" of particular value in developing understanding on the part of both parents and children. I would hasten to add that the value of this technique presupposes, of course, that the problem is not complicated by personality variables other than the ones which are found in the normal family relationship.

8...

He Had No Family

Rob was a student in a state school for boys where admission was dependent upon either one or both parents being deceased. My own position was that of placement director for the boys. This involved finding positions for the boys upon graduation from the school and also entailed a limited amount of counseling.

Rob initiated counseling in the fall of his junior year and continued on an irregular basis until his graduation the following year. When Rob first came in, he was actively seeking reassurance and support in his relationships with both his father and step-mother. While Rob was not a serious adjustment problem in school, he frequently sought activities which would enable him to be excused from his classes. He apparently gained prestige for himself by finding jobs which needed to be done, asking permission to do them, and then telling his teachers that Mr. ——— needed him to do some work. His school work was average and was in line with what might be expected from our psychometric data.

Rob was an illegitimate child. However, Rob's father had assumed responsibility for the boy and had attempted to help him since the death of the boy's mother. Rob's mother had married several times after the boy was born, and Rob had led a rather unhappy life. When Rob was twelve years old, his mother had died of a heart condition aggravated by alcoholism. For several years after his mother's death, Rob was shuttled from pillar to post and was forced to live with a number of people who were not interested in him. Eventually Rob's father took him into his home; however, his wife did not get along with, nor did she like, the boy.

Rob was unaware of the condition of his birth. Further he did not know that his father was, in fact, his real father. His mother had placed a fictitious name on his birth certificate. His step-mother, although aware of the situation, refused to let anyone broach the subject. She referred to Rob's father as an adoptive father. Apparently this gave her moral dominance over her husband. She, herself, was childless, and she seemed to gain satisfaction by rejecting the boy and making life miserable for his father. This rejecting home situation had aggravated and increased Rob's resentment and frustration. He was obviously concerned about the fact that his family did not demonstrate an interest in him. Their attitude had created a sense of aloneness in Rob and had caused him to doubt his worth as an individual. Although he believed his father was seriously concerned about his welfare, he expressed resentment and hostility towards his family.

Counseling

Even though the counseling which I was able to do was limited in nature, I attempted to help Rob reassess his potential. I placed particular emphasis upon his strengths. Secondly, I attempted to encourage Rob to express his hostility freely and made no attempt to censure or evaluate his expressions. Lastly, I attempted to help Rob accept the situation as one which was not likely to change.

Contact between Rob and his parents increased during the last few months of his senior year; however, there was no apparent change in their relationship. For this reason I attempted to help Rob make plans which were independent of his home. He seemed to accept, at least on the intellectual level, this planning.

Shortly before graduation a last counseling session was scheduled which included Rob and his family. I hoped that this session would convince Rob, beyond all doubt, that he would have to make his plans independently and that he could not count on parental help. Rob's father started out the session by stating that he wanted Rob to come home upon graduation and that he was looking forward to the occasion. Then Rob's step-mother launched into a lecture on working. She said that life was not a "bowl-of-cherries." There were certain things to be done such as associating with the right kind of people, not staying out to all hours, and so forth. Rob, who had talked easily at the beginning of the session when things were on a "greeting basis," retired into a shell of brooding silence. He finally asked to be excused, and I permitted him to leave.

I brought the session to a close by making one last attempt to help Rob's parents understand the situation. I told them that there was no doubt in my mind that Robert had real affection for both of them. I went on to say that for the last several years Rob had been questioning his importance in their lives, that it had become increasingly difficult for him to accept the fact that he was not visited as often as his friends, and that special occasions such as birthdays and Christmas came and went without any remembrance from home. I pointed out that our records revealed that Rob had received only one visit in the four years he had been in our school and that their letters had been limited to only a few notes, mostly in the last several months. I went on to say, "Rob does not complain about this, but he has run out of explanations to himself as to why he does not receive more visits and communications from home. Because Rob does not understand your actions, he seems to have become increasingly convinced that you are not interested in him, and he is afraid to express his interest in you for fear of being hurt." I told them that I had talked with Rob in an attempt to help him understand and accept his situation without becoming bitter. However, I did not believe that Rob understood or would ever understand why he was not wanted at home. I concluded by saying that this was a crucial period in Rob's life, that he was filled with self doubts, and that he did not know where he belonged or where he was wanted.

Rob's step-mother dominated the remainder of the interview. She made a few apologetic remarks, but then went on to make a number of negative comments about Rob's attitude and what she would expect of him if he returned home. Finally, Rob's father told his wife to "shut-up." He apologized to me and said that my remarks made sense and that he and his wife would have to sit down and straighten out their problems and relationships with Rob. I could not help but feel that very little had been accomplished in our talk and that the home situation would continue to be an impossible one.

I reached the conclusion that Rob should be placed outside of his home community and made my plans accordingly. I secured an interview for him with a small manufacturing company. He made a favorable impression and was given a trainee position, the job of assistant to the manager. After about two weeks on the job, I received the report that he was not accepting his job responsibilities and was doing his work in a careless manner. Because of his ability to win friends, he was kept on the job for another month and then released. Even at the time of his dismissal, his employer was impressed with his "potential."

Rob immediately secured another position as a sales clerk. My last report from his employer mentions that Rob is, at times, careless in his work and avoids assuming responsibility. The employer has spoken to Rob about this, and Rob continues to hold the job; however, I wonder how long he will be employed.

Discussion

I believe that Rob has developed some insight into the fact that he will not be accepted by his family. I do not believe that he has yet gained adequate emotional acceptance of this fact. Probably much of the friendly and impressive veneer which Rob displays to his employers is a manifestation of his attempt to be accepted. Perhaps Rob will go through a period of "job hopping" and then finally will settle down. However, I am inclined to believe that it is very likely that Rob will go from one job to another for most of his life. If he is fortunate, he may find a place for himself. However, until he is able to accept himself, he will continue to be unacceptable to others.

I do not believe that Rob's family situation will ever improve to the degree that he will gain the emotional support which he needs. While his father has a fair understanding of his son's problem, his step-mother is not likely to change. I do not think that she will ever be able to accept Rob because of her own personality deficiencies, and Rob's threat to her as the illegitimate child of her husband.

The amount of counseling which I did with Rob was relatively superficial. In my position I was unable to devote any amount of counseling time to him. However, I have wondered, if adequate counseling facilities had been available, whether Rob would have gained security by knowing that his father was his *real* father. I realize that this knowledge might also have caused some other problems; yet, perhaps Rob would have felt that he really belonged to someone though his father was not able to take him back into his home. I also wonder what the effect of the release of this secret would be upon the relationship between Rob's father and his wife.

9...
I Tried To Buy
Friends For
My Child

Sandra was first tested by the school psychologist when she was in the fifth grade. On the Wechsler Intelligence Scale for Children, Sandra had a Verbal I.Q. of 79, a Performance I.Q. of 93, and a Full Scale I.Q. of 84. It was recommended that Sandra be placed in a class for slow learners.

Sandra was not a physically attractive child. She had irregular teeth which protruded slightly, wore glasses, and her hearing ability had been questioned. Upon being examined for the latter defect, only a very slight loss could be found. Sandra had also undergone speech training for four years. Her speech was now understandable but still differed noticeably from the other children. At the insistence of her mother, Sandra had started school a year early. Her failure had caused both mother and child considerable embarrassment. Sandra's father was an artist who was considered tempermental and apparently had little patience with the child.

Counseling

When Sandra came into my office, she gave the impression of being a childish, immature youngster. Although chronologically in early adolescence, her behavior belied the fact. She was somewhat passive and seemed susceptive to nervous sieges of giggling. Sandra spoke of her mother warmly but appeared to be somewhat afraid of her father. She expressed the desire to become a secretary.

45

As Sandra's mother had come with her, I spoke to her alone after Sandra had returned to class. Sandra's mother, understandably concerned about her daughter, gave the impression of being extremely over-protective and furthermore showed little real understanding of her daughter's condition. From her statements I learned that Sandra had been a full term baby but that during the last five months of pregnancy, her mother had been very sick and had had frequent hemorrhages. Sandra began to walk at 14 months but was late in talking. When she was four weeks old, she had a "choking spell," turned blue, and was thought to have died. During the following two years, she had convulsions every time she had a fever. Sandra also had pneumonia several times and a severe kidney infection. Until recently she complained of pains in the stomach which were accompanied by profuse perspiration and incoherent talk.

Sandra's mother indicated that she has tried to make her daughter become a socially popular young lady. She said that she felt that Sandra's problem was that she wanted to be accepted, "was very sensitive," and suffered when she made comparisons between herself and other girls her age. Her mother thought that Sandra's biggest concern was that she had no friends. For some time she had been playing with four- and five-year-old children. Her father demanded that this practice cease. Sandra's mother told me that she had tried to buy friends for her child. That is to say, she had had weekly parties to which children were invited. However, soon after this practice started, the children either refused to come or did not appear when they were invited. These parties had become a neighborhood topic, and Sandra was very embarrassed about the talk.

When the subject of school placement came up, Sandra's mother refused to believe that her child was "slow." She, at first, placed the blame upon Sandra's poor hearing and speech difficulty. She insisted on taking the child to other professional people to be checked.

Sandra's mother came back with a radical shift in viewpoint. She now wanted to place Sandra in an institution. Rather than attempting change this attitude, I suggested that we have Sandra examined at Out Patient Clinic of the State Mental Hospital. I hoped, by this, btain the opinions of experts whom Sandra's mother would re- The hospital report indicated that Sandra's difficulty stemmed organic cause; probably, the result of prolonged cerebral anoxia at the age of four weeks and the convulsive seizures in the next several years. Sandra was also given an intelligence test, and her I.Q. was reported as being 62. The report went on to say that the staff did not feel that Sandra needed institutional care. She could be handled quite adequately by receiving understanding in her home environment and by being placed in a special education class.

I reviewed the results of the hospital report with Sandra's mother. I pointed out to her that it was possible that Sandra's many illnesses had caused her to develop an over-protective attitude towards the child. I discussed with her how Sandra's working under pressure, and being placed in situations where failure was inevitable, had contributed to the child's present nervous state. Her mother acknowledged that she knew that Sandra had feigned illness at times to keep from doing her schoolwork. She went on to say that she now realized what she had been doing and that she would allow the child to be placed in a special education class. She added that she would also permit her daughter to make her own friends within the new group.

Reports from Sandra's teacher over the past three months have shown an increasing relaxation on the part of the child. She has made several friends in her class and is actively participating in her schoolwork. She has developed an interest in art, which in turn, has caused a closer relationship to develop between Sandra and her father. Sandra's mother has kept her word and seems to have accepted Sandra for what she is rather than attempting to make Sandra into something she is not.

Discussion

A common problem for counselors who work with retarded children is the problem of developing parental acceptance. As can be observed from Sandra's case, it was her mother who needed the counseling. I am quite certain that Sandra's mother was cognizant of the fact that her child was retarded. However, she had not been able to accept this emotionally until she had exhausted every open avenue of explanation. It is difficult for parents, particularly in high social positions, to accept the fact that their child will not be able to win a place for himself at the desired status level. The counselor who works with such parents will need to accept the fact that his own motives, intelligence, and sanity will be frequently questioned by well meaning but emotionally blind parents. These parents will frequently blame others, often the counselor, for what they cannot accept themselves. It is as if they were saying, "It must be someone's fault that my child is as she is. It can't be my fault." Of course, the truth of the matter is that frequently the parent may feel deeply, that she is the cause of the child's condition. The counselor will need to understand that the acceptance of a retarded child for many parents will be a most painful process.

10...

My Parents Don't Want Me

Bill is a twelve-year-old, seventh-grade boy whose mental maturity and standardized achievement test scores indicate superior ability. He was first brought to my attention, as a counselor, by his teachers who were concerned because his grades were low in comparison to what the psychometric data and other observations indicated they should be. The teachers also stated that he was becoming something of a discipline problem. He was not a problem in the sense that he wilfully violated the rules of the school and the classroom. It was rather, according to his teachers, that his behavior seemed odd. Comments from his teachers included such remarks as: "Makes spontaneous inappropriate remarks. . . . Full of nervous energy. . . . Always runs. . . . Can't seem to get along with other students. . . . Seeks my time and attention at most awkward times. . . . Spends much time drawing and daydreaming in class." In short, they felt that he was desperately seeking to be noticed and recognized. As I began to observe him, I quite agreed with their evaluation; but I did not feel that he was cognizant of his behavior.

Shortly after I began to observe Bill more closely, the school nurse and his homeroom teacher came to me almost simultaneously. The nurse reported that he had come to her on three successive days at about two o'clock complaining of stomach cramps and nausea. His homeroom teacher reported that he was beginning to come to school late and to be absent frequently. I made a point to "accidentally" place myself where I could meet Bill and begin to become acquainted with him. After several days of arranging to be at places where I could greet him and talk with him for a few moments, I asked the nurse to send him to me the next time he came to her.

Two days later he reported to the nurse again. After examining him, she sent him to me. I talked with him for a short time, long enough to feel that he was afraid to go home for some reason. As he was unwilling to talk about it, I did not press him. Instead we spent most of the session getting to know each other. He did tell me that his tardiness and absences were because he had to get up, dress, prepare his own breakfast, make his school lunch, and sometimes care for his younger brother. His mother and father refused to get out of bed until it was time for his younger brother to go to kindergarten. In fact, Bill said that if he disturbed them at all his mother became furiously angry. After this session his absences and tardiness became less frequent, and he no longer went to the nurse. However, his teachers reported that his work was slipping badly and his behavior was getting worse.

About two weeks later, his mother came to see me at the end of a parent conference day at school. She wanted to arrange for a mathematics tutor for Bill. In the light of later events, it might be well to describe this woman. From Bill's folder and from his teachers' comments, I thought I had some idea of what to expect. I was hardly prepared! She came into my office looking like something out of a Dali painting. Brilliant blue, tight toreador pants; a blazing orange-checked blouse; eye and facial makeup, so vivid as to be almost hideous; and coal-black lacquered hair gave an almost blinding effect. I would describe her attitude as defensively hostile.

After she informed me of the purpose of her visit, I said that the school was quite concerned about Bill's academic achievement. She said that she realized his work left something to be desired and that she thought she knew the reason for this. As she talked, she said that she felt Bill was emotionally disturbed, probably because of her. She concluded by saying, "I had a few appointments with a guidance clinic; but when it became apparent that it was only going to be unpleasant for me, I stopped going. I realize that whatever is wrong with him is probably my fault, but I have decided that I am the way I am. I can't change, and Bill will have to live with this."

At the end of the interview, she did say that she would be willing to try any suggestions I might have to help Bill. I made a few, very simple suggestions only to discover later that none of them were ever tried out at home.

After this interview with Bill's mother, I felt that it was time for Bill and me to get down to serious business before his school situation deteriorated any further. A few days later I called him to my office. I told him that I was concerned about his school work and that I felt he was not doing as well as he should or could do. In the course of our conversation, he asked me about "all those tests the school gave." I got out his folder and interpreted his scores with him. He did not seem surprised or elated when I said that they indicated good ability and that his teachers and I believed that he had a great deal to offer. He said that he also believed he could do better, knew that he was not doing as well as he should, but did not know what caused this. He went on to say that he wanted to talk with me again to see what we could do.

A Critical Counseling Session

In the next two weeks, Bill and I had about six sessions together. I found him very willing to talk, but only on a superficial basis. He talked about school, his previous school, his teachers, his interests, his classes, and various happenings in and out of school. At times he would begin talking about his home and family, and then suddenly he would change the subject. If, at these times, I would ask a question or try to clarify a statement, he would become very evasive and burst forth with what appeared to be a cover-up of nervous speech. I began to feel that Bill knew what was driving him to seek attention and was hindering the progress of his work, and that he wanted to talk about it; however, he just could not bring himself to do so. I felt that, if Bill was to do anything with the rest of the year, we would have to bring this problem out into the open and face it together.

At the end of the seventh session, I said, "Bill, you have a lot of talent, a great deal of ability and a great amount to contribute to the school. I would hate to see your talent and ability go to waste. I like you and I want to help. I have enjoyed our discussions, but somehow I feel that there is something that you think you should tell me and can't bring yourself to do it. If I am right, you think this over and decide whether or not you would like to discuss it tomorrow."

At this point Bill broke down completely. He put his head down in his hands and began to sob violently. I remained quiet for a period of time to allow him to regain his composure. Finally he said, "There is something, but I don't know if I should tell you." I asked him why he didn't want to tell me, and he said that he was afraid that I would think it was ridiculous. I told him that I wanted to help and that if it was important to him and could affect his school work and upset him that much, then it couldn't be ridiculous. Again he was wracked by sobs and went completely to pieces.

I remained silent while he cried for about five minutes. When I thought he had become calm enough to understand what I was saying, I said, "You don't have to tell me anything until you are ready." He said that he did want to talk about it, but he just couldn't. He tried to say more, mumbled some inarticulate words, but couldn't go on. I had the thought that he might be embarrassed at breaking down in front of me, so I said, "Suppose I leave the office for about five minutes. When I come back, if you are ready to talk about it, we'll talk. If not today, then whenever you are ready. You will also find paper and pencil on the bookcase. If you feel that perhaps you would like to write down your thoughts, feel free to do so." Bill nodded his head in agreement and I left. I made certain on my way out to the outer office that the secretary, who knew he was there, would see he was not disturbed by the telephone or intercom system.

When I returned, he had completely regained his composure and appeared calm and poised. He had a sheet of paper and a pencil in front of him. He had written nothing; but as soon as I closed the door he said, "I feel that I would like to talk about it now if you don't mind." I told him that I would be more than happy to listen to him. He then said, "It's about my mother and father." At this he began to cry again, but he continued in a halting fashion: "I don't think that they love me." After a long pause, he continued, "In fact, sometimes I don't think they even want me." It took a good two minutes for him to get these two comments out.

After he had said this, I could almost feel him relax and his tremendous relief was obvious. He then continued with his story of a relationship at home which appears to be completely devoid of affection for him. His comments were mostly about his mother of whom he is deathly afraid. She is apparently extremely inconsistent in her behavior and administers physical punishment at the slightest provocation. She is fanatical about the housework, all of which Bill has to do every day, very harsh in her treatment of Bill, and obviously partial to his younger brother. Bill reported that she shows violent displays of temper toward him and that she never seems to be sorry when she injures him or ruins any of his possessions. She has torn up his homework, thrown his school books and a desk lamp at him, and has refused to let him show any affection to his brother. Bill does not seem to resent his brother although he gets by far the best treatment. Bill's mother also ridicules his efforts, cannot understand why he has no friends, and why he is not getting good grades. On top of all this, she has even forbidden him to volunteer any contributions in class recitation periods.

Without any solicitation on my part, I have since talked with people who know the family, but do not know of my work with Bill. From these comments, I have no reason to suppose that Bill has exaggerated his situation. Bill's father appears to be a rather vague figure whose major role in life seems to be keeping out of the path of his wife. I suppose it is pointless to note that Bill's mother might profit from some rather extensive therapy. Regardless of this, I do not believe that there is much point in working with her about Bill. At this writing, I am trying to arrange a meeting with Bill's father.

Since the session described, I have learned from Bill's teachers that he is much less of a problem in class. They also report that Bill seems much more secure and confident and is developing better relationships with his classmates. Although still far from what it should be, his work is improving. Bill has a great amount of talent in the area of art, especially cartooning. Through this he seems to have developed a good relationship with his art teacher. Feeling that this relationship could help Bill, I have explained the situation to this teacher. She reports that he often comes to see her after school, and she now encourages this. She is trying to go out of her way to be a friend to him. This relationship appears to be working out well.

I am seeing Bill once or twice a week or whenever he wants to come in and "unload." At the present he is still confused and cannot understand his relationship with his mother. I have been trying to reassure him that we will try to do everything that we can to help at school. I have also been trying to help him understand his mother's actions and to accept her as she is. He appears to be adjusting more readily and is not as easily upset by his mother's behavior. His periods of depression, which result from his mother's actions, do not seem to last as long. His teachers still report that they can tell when something unpleasant has happened at home from his actions in school. They are aware of the general situation and are trying to be understanding.

Discussion

I feel that some progress has been made in this case. Probably the major factor in Bill's improvement was the emotional relief he gained in sharing his problem with me. I believe that his improvement will continue and that time and maturity will be in his favor. This case does bring some questions to my mind. In a situation such as this, to what extent should a school counselor attempt to develop a youngster's understanding that his mother (or father) has emotional problems which prevent her from acting normally? I don't see much hope for an improvement in the family situation. Bill's only hope, in my opinion, is to live with the situation and to try to understand it. I also wonder why Bill's mother favors the younger boy. Bill hasn't mentioned this, but I don't know what I would answer if he should. I would also like to point out how extremely necessary it is for a counselor to have the respect and cooperation of the faculty and administration in his school. I am certain that my ability to develop a close relationship with Bill in such a relatively short period of time and the increasingly favorable outcome of the situation can, to a large extent, be credited to all of us working together. In conclusion, I wonder if there are any general rules that one can extract from a case such as this that will help other youngsters like Bill. Is there more that I could have done? Is there more that I should be doing now? Could the situation be handled better?

11...

A One Man Wrecking Crew

Mac, age thirteen, came to our school in the seventh grade. He was seen innumerable times by his counselor, chiefly because of behavioral problems in the classroom. Mac had been in trouble with practically every teacher in the school. He appeared in his counselor's office almost daily to correct some "injustice" done to him or because he had been in trouble. Mac impressed his counselor as being most unstable and full of misdirected energy.

Mac was a poor student, low in measured intellectual ability (Wechsler Bellevue Full Scale I.Q. of 69), and had definite antisocial tendencies. He was unable to get along with his peers and they, in turn, shied away from him. One of his classes even got up a petition to have him removed from their section. They stated that his language and behavior, in and out of class, had harmed them as a group.

Mac talked freely with his counselor; he stated that he had lots of difficulties out of school as well as in school. He volunteered the information that he had been investigated by the F.B.I. in Georgia for having placed railroad ties on the train track. He also said that he once held up a woman with a toy cap pistol. Mac delivered this information in a voice which was devoid of affect. He did not seem to realize either the inappropriateness of his actions or the possible dangers involved. Mac added that he felt that people picked on him and that he got far more punishment for what he did than what other individuals would receive for the same actions.

Several attempts had been made to give Mac constructive jobs from which he could receive satisfaction. He was placed on the school safety patrol but had to be removed as he started trouble so that he could bring students to the office to show his authority. Mac had a good singing voice, and he was asked to participate in a school talent show. He was not permitted to sing when he came to school the day before the program with an "outlandish" haircut. He had had his hair closely cropped, and this became a source of conversation for everyone who saw him. It also presented a discipline problem for Mac resented the remarks which were made and was more than willing to fight. In fact, the fights were numerous enough to initiate suspension proceedings. Before he could be suspended, he came into school with two shaven places on his head. He stated that these were horns and that he was trying to look like Mephistopheles. Mac was suspended, and a letter was written to his parents stating that they should bring him to school after his hair had grown back in.

When Mac returned to school, his mother came with him. The counselor learned that Mac's father had died and that since his death she had remarried twice. Mac had a younger brother by the second marriage and a sister by the last one. Mac's mother also stated that her present husband had walked out on her and that now she was contemplating a divorce. During this interview she disclosed that she had difficulty in controlling Mac and was at her wit's end as to what to do about his behavior. The counselor told her that he could see there were home difficulties about which to be concerned. "But how did she think Mac could adjust to the conflicts and tensions within his home if she were so frustrated as an adult?" Mac's mother said that she had tried to help Mac, but that he had told her on numerous occasions that, to him, women were insignificant creatures. She also said that she was very frightened of Mac because he was so big and strong for his age. Once he had threatened to kill her at the point of a gun when she had reprimanded him for his behavior. Another time he threatened to throw her down the cellar stairs if she didn't leave him alone.

Fortunately, Mac did have a favorable side. There was general agreement that, at most times, he appeared generally pleasant and would have liked to have been helpful. Even if it meant staying after school, he volunteered his services for the school faculty. Mac seemed to like school but didn't realize how annoying he was to other people. He was not able to understand that he was wrong many times. Although he had a temper, his counselor did not think that under normal conditions he would harm anyone.

Mac was referred to the school psychologist. After administering a diagnostic battery of tests, the psychologist concluded that Mac's school achievement appeared to be close to his ability level. However, his motivation for academic work was low, and this was manifested in his destructive tendencies. Mac seemed to enjoy taking the Thematic Apperception Test. His stories were filled with physical violence. Frequently the central figure in the picture was injured in some manner but recovered and went on to have a successful future. Mac showed some difficulty in sexual identification in his stories. Most of his stories involved conflict with the law. However, the characters were always apprehended, punished, and rehabilitated.

Conclusion

Because of Mac's poor adjustment in his regular classes and his low achievement, his counselor recommended that he be placed in a special education class. This was to take place when Mac returned from a second suspension. As a result of this second suspension, Mac had to appear before a judge of the Juvenile Court. Because of Mac's past history, the judge recommended that Mac be given a neuro-psychiatric evaluation at the state hospital. The question was how to get Mac to the hospital without causing a further disturbance.

When Mac returned to school, his counselor called him into the office. He told Mac that the school felt that he might be able to produce more satisfactory work if he were placed in the special education group. Mac seemed pleased and said, "Now I might get better grades."

The next problem was to get him to the state hospital for an examination. His counselor, remembering that Mac took an interest in singing, told him that there were some men who were going to put on a program at the hospital for the patients. These men were going to use some of the more talented children in Mac's school for the program. The counselor inquired if Mac would be interested in participating. He was! The counselor then called the hospital and contacted the physician who would be evaluating Mac. He told him the method he had used to get Mac to the hospital and also made an appointment for the boy.

Psychiatric assessment of Mac found him seriously disturbed. He had impaired reality controls and schizophrenic-like distortions. These findings suggested a serious emotional disturbance. They found Mac fearful of his own thoughts and indicated that hostility was expressed in his aggressive outbursts. The final outcome of Mac's case was that he was placed in a school for emotionally disturbed boys.

Discussion

I have chosen Mac's case to discuss for several reasons. I believe a number of mistakes were made and that something can be learned from these mistakes.

First of all, I don't think that any counseling was done with Mac. The only function which the counselor served was as a place to send Mac when he became too much for his teachers. The counselor, himself, was unable to establish any relationship with Mac which was beneficial in nature. I think that this was partly due to inadequate training and, consequently, inadequate understanding. The second reason for the lack of rapport was that the counselor viewed Mac as a problem rather than a boy with a problem. The counselor's main goal was to change Mac's behavior so that he would no longer be a problem for the school, rather than to help Mac to understand and to change his own behavior so that he would no longer be a problem to himself. Having observed this counselor, I would guess that he tends to be quite directive in his comments and would be likely to monopolize the counseling session. An example of this is the inappropriate comment to Mac's mother. For Mac, the counselor was but a long extension of the law, the school, and other authority figures. Mac had not found one understanding person in his short life. I believe that this counselor might have accomplished something beneficial if he had attempted to be an accepting and understanding person.

There were sufficient signs in Mac's behavior to indicate the necessity of referral long before it was initiated. While a skilled counselor might have been of some supportive help, Mac needed a more intensive therapeutic relationship than is normally available in the public school. Also, the decision to place Mac in a special education class should have been made much earlier. It is difficult for me to believe that it was possible for Mac to go through seven years of schooling without having this problem identified; yet, it happened.

Finally, the subterfuge used to get Mac to the neuro-psychiatric evaluation seems to me to be most unethical. I believe that it was used because the counselor did not have the courage to calmly tell Mac of his need for such an examination. I am sure that it is seldom, if ever, justifiable to lie to a counselee.

In summary, I feel that the school could have done much more to aid Mac. Although the school can never be held accountable for the home environment of a child, it is responsible for the identification of problems which interfere with the child's functioning in the classroom. If, at an earlier date, Mac had been put in an academic program which suited his abilities and if he had been better understood by the adults who came into contact with him, it is quite possible that Mac would not have had to enter a school for the emotionally disturbed.

12...
A Case For Referral

Eddy was first referred to the Guidance Office by his French teacher. In her letter she stated:

Until Eddy came in one day after school to make up a test, I had really no impression of him at all. In class he is extremely quiet; he speaks when called on and even then he is reluctant. He is attentive and does good written work; his report mark was "A". When I spoke to him alone, he told me a great deal about himself. He is intelligent, but self-conscious and very nervous. He has been absent quite a few times, apparently because he worries so much about his studies that he gets sick. He states that he does not sleep well. He has few, if any, friends in school and feels inadequate because he has been moved into the top section of his class this year. The fact that he is physically small bothers him. He has read a great deal and is well informed about many subjects. However, he is quite immature emotionally. He keeps repeating that he is different from other people and is proud to be so; however, this seems to be merely a cover-up for an underlying desire to be accepted by boys and girls his own age. I feel that Eddy needs a great deal of help and understanding that I would like, but am not qualified, to give. I wonder if professional help might not be advisable.

As Eddy's guidance counselor, I called him in to discuss his sickness. I found that he had been absent some thirteen days in the semester. Eddy reiterated the same general remarks that he had made in his discussion with his French teacher. I suggested that we have some further interviews. Eddy readily acquiesced.

A week later Eddy's father called me stating that his son's behavior had become stranger than ever before; that he felt he should bring it to our attention. Because of his excessive sickness, which seemed invariably to occur on test days, the school nurse had also talked with me about Eddy. I called Eddy in for a second interview. He was sarcastic, flippant, and defensive. He proceeded to state that if he was supposed to be crazy, he was going to act crazy. He began a strange dialogue which went like this:

"Have you met the Prince of Darkness?"
"I don't know."
"Well, he's all around you. Are you sure you haven't met him?"
"How would I recognize him?"
"You don't recognize him; he recognizes you."
"Well, what are his signs?"
"He gives you sleep and quiet. He brings the night. But you can't see him (Here Eddy pointed at the center of the desk which was empty) because he's invisible. Do I sound crazy? Do you think I'm crazy?"

Eddy continued to ask whether I thought that he was "crazy." I did not reflect any conclusions about his mental status to him, but I did become apprehensive about his behavior.

In the course of subsequent interviews, Eddy gave me further information about himself. He stated that he felt that he was becoming physically weaker and was concerned about his loss of weight and what he considered to be an attendant loss of strength. He was upset about his physical appearance and considered himself an unattractive person. He disliked the color of his hair, the nature of his teeth, and his physical height. He did not wear his glasses because he felt that they would detract from his appearance. Eddy placed an inordinate amount of emphasis upon academic achievement. He talked constantly about his school work and the need to do well. He depreciated the other students in his class on the ground that, though they did better than he, they differed markedly because they did not really "think." They were better students but lacked the insight and background of knowledge that he had. His conversation centered about the need to be accepted by these other students in his class and his need to achieve on their level.

The previous year Eddy had been in a lower academic section. However, this year due to the insistence of both Eddy and his parents, he had been moved to the highest academic group. We have the following data on Eddy:

Psychometric and Coursework Data

Iowa Tests of Educational Development(Local Norms)

	Percentile
Background in Social Studies	78
Background in Natural Science	64
Quantitative Thinking	45
Reading in Social Science	81
Reading in Literature	65
General Vocabulary	71
Composite Score for the Entire Test	73

Lorge-Thorndike Intelligence Test (Level 4)
Verbal I.Q.	113
Non Verbal I.Q.	101
Total I.Q.	107

Differential Aptitude Tests (National Norms)

	Percentile
Verbal	85
Numerical	90
Abstract	75
Spatial	75
Mechanical	80
Clerical	50
Spelling	75
Sentences	80

Eddy was absent nine days last year, and his grades were as follows:

English I	B
Social Studies	A—
Latin I	B+
Algebra I	B—
Mechanical Drwg.	C—
Health	B
Physical Educ.	B

During the first six weeks of this year, Eddy has been absent thirteen times, and his grades are as follows:

English II	B
Latin II	A
French I	A
Algebra II	C+
Biology	C
Health	A
Physical Educ.	C

Prior to coming to our high school, Eddy attended a church school belonging to one of the fundamentalist sects. When we discussed this aspect of his school experience, Eddy stated that it was a one-room school. His teacher had been "saved" and therefore included a great deal of religious instruction in the course of study. Eddy felt that his teacher had not been very adequate. However, Eddy stated that he had received a superior education compared with the education offered him in the public schools. He said that he was glad that he had attended this religious school rather than a public school. When I asked him how he accounted for the better grades of the public school children in his class, he stated that it was due to his failure in health.

Our school nurse, who is also a trained social worker, has interviewed Eddy's parents in their home. She reports that the conditions of the home are quite average. Eddy was a full term baby, walked and talked within the normal time, and had the usual childhood diseases. There are three other children in the family: an older married sister, an older brother who is in the Navy, and a brother who is fourteen and one year younger than Eddy. Eddy has had difficulty with one of his eyes. This was corrected by treatment and glasses at the age of three.

The parents explained to the nurse that since June of this year, Eddy had complained of an upset stomach. Eddy's father took him to the family physician. He was given a physical examination but no abnormalities were found. Since the condition still persisted, Eddy was again taken to the doctor in October. At this time the physician prescribed a mild sedative to be taken in the evening and before bedtime. This seemed to help for almost a week; after that Eddy was much the same as before. Eddy ate very little. He nibbled at his food, seldom stayed seated long enough to complete a meal. Eddy was very particular about his appearance and refused to wear any second-hand clothes. He took care of his own room and everything was orderly and neat. He did not like to go downtown and would not answer the telephone or the door.

I referred Eddy to our visiting school psychologist when I decided that his problem was more severe than the result of just being placed in a higher academic group or a minor emotional upset. In his initial interview with Eddy, the psychologist had a brief talk with him and then administered the Minnesota Multiphasic Personality Inventory and a Sentence Completion Test. In the course of their conversation, Eddy stated that he was having trouble with his stomach. He felt that he was "floating like an amoeba."

The psychologist interpreted Eddy's personality test scores as follows:

Eddy has scores high above the modal range in the areas of depression, psychasthenia, and hypochondriasis. There is a high schizophrenia score which should be interpreted cautiously as it may be derived from the other three high scores. These scores fit in with the expressed complaints of mental exhaustion and physical symptoms, coupled with anxiety in stress situations. Two other scores, but still above the modal range, tie in with the total picture. These scores are in the hysteria and paranoia areas. There is a possibility that all scores are somewhat heightened by Eddy's excessive conscientiousness and hypersensitivity to his own feelings; however, the pattern remains. The results of the sentence completion test suggest feelings of depression, anxiety, confusion, difficulty in concentration, the desire to escape from pressures, feelings of physical and emotional fatigue, and high standards of achievement.

I arranged for a staff conference which included the nurse, the principal, several of Eddy's teachers and the psychologist. Out of this conference came the following recommendations:

1. Reduce Eddy's academic load by dropping one subject in the mathematics or science area. In the final outcome of the case, we permitted Eddy to audit his biology course but relieved him from taking examinations. He was told that he would not receive credit for the course this year but could, if he wished, take the course for credit

some other year. This decision was made in order to spare Eddy from losing face with his peers and, at the same time, to encourage him for future work in the sciences.

2. We recommended a psychiatric appraisal to determine whether the degree of neurotic behavior manifested was severe enough to require further treatment beyond a reduction in class load. With respect to this recommendation, Eddy was referred to the community psychiatric clinic for treatment.

3. We recommended that the referral to the psychiatrist be subject to the approval of Eddy's family doctor. Eddy's physician was whole-heartedly in agreement with our suggestion.

Discussion

Eddy was not a counseling case for a school counselor. The school counselor will, however, have the responsibility of identifying children with personality problems, and may, occasionally, act in a supporting role while the case is being processed. To some extent I believe our school precipitated Eddy's difficulties by acquiescing to home pressures and placing Eddy in an advanced section of his class. From an examination of the psychometric data which we have on Eddy, it is apparent to me that Eddy is over-achieving in school. I believe that if Eddy had been kept in the lower, but above average, section of last year, the environmental pressures would have been much less. Possibly Eddy would have been able to master his emotional problems. Frankly, I do not understand all of the underlying personality dynamics in Eddy's case. Perhaps school counselors should be given better training in this area. My own training has been inadequate, but I have the feeling that Eddy's problem should have been recognized earlier. Too frequently the quiet child in the classroom is overlooked because he is not causing any trouble. If our school had recognized earlier that Eddy was a troubled youngster, remedial action might have been initiated long before it was, thus correcting or preventing what happened to Eddy.

13...

Supportive
Counseling

Karen is a fourteen-year-old student in a residential school for the blind. She has limited vision which is insufficient for reading but permits her to distinguish the forms of objects. Karen's family life can be characterized as being plagued with difficulties. Her father is a conscientious and responsible individual; however, his work prevents him from remaining at home for any lengthy period of time. Although at the present time she is home, her mother has been a patient at a state mental hospital. Karen's younger sister is also a student in our school for the blind, and her two younger brothers have been placed in foster homes.

Karen and her sister began their education in a school for the blind in a neighboring state. Transfer records indicate that Karen has low normal intelligence as measured by the verbal section of the Wechsler Intelligence Scale. This finding has been supported from several administrations of the test over a five-year period. Her records also indicate that she is a nervous, socially retarded child who requires continual encouragement. In school she has done fairly good work although she takes longer to complete her work than most children. She seems to do the best in spelling and geography and has the most difficulty with language and science. Karen has trouble getting along with the other children. She explains this trouble by saying, "Most kids accuse me of things I don't do."

It is of interest to note that, in a psychological testing situation, Karen is energetic and appears to enjoy being the center of attention. However, when she does not grasp the task immediately, she becomes resistant and complains that the test is a "dumb game" and slows down. It appears that she does this purposefully. The results of a short objective personality inventory confirm the many observations which have been accumulated concerning Karen's behavior. She is an introverted person who has little understanding of herself and little concern for others. She tends to be domineering and inconsiderate. She does not understand the reactions of others and lives in an imaginative world of her own creation.

Throughout the past year Karen was the subject of a number of staff meetings. She was quite definitely a behavior problem for she had been involved in numerous fights with her classmates and was given to uncontrollable tantrums and hysterics. She became so antagonistic towards her teachers that her school work suffered. A few of her teachers were able to develop temporary good relationships with Karen and reported that she could be best handled by being spoken to in a quiet but firm voice. There were times, they felt, when she could not be reached because she was not in contact with reality. At the end of the school year, it was agreed that psychiatric treatment should be sought for Karen.

At the beginning of the new school year, I requested the results of the psychiatric counseling. It had been most superficial in nature and consisted of an evaluation which was in essential agreement with the psychologist's report from our own institution. Upon further inquiry I learned that there was no possibility of any other psychiatric referral; and, therefore, it was apparent that if Karen was to be helped, she would have to be helped within our institution.

Karen and I were acquainted since we had worked together for a brief period of time during the prior school year. She was quite happy to see me; and I structured the conference, as I had with the other students, by explaining to her that we were setting up a counseling program this year which enabled me to be available on certain days for conference. I explained that she would not be given any more tests but that we would talk about any topic or any problems which arose during the year. She seemed agreeable to this arrangement. To start the conversation, I asked her how her summer had gone. She replied that it was a terrible summer for her because her mother did not understand her and had been very mean and unfair. Her mother always took her sister's side against her and seemed to hate her. From our records I knew that there was some truth in what Karen was saying, and I listened quietly without comment.

At the next counseling session, we talked about her school relationships. She realized that she had trouble in controlling her temper and had become "quite sick over it." She blamed most of this on her teachers and housemother who misunderstood her and on her classmates who hated her. She said that she would try to control her temper this year and thought she would be able to if "only people wouldn't scream at me and stir me up."

As we were attempting a program to enrich the intellectual development of the children, I suggested to Karen that perhaps she might like to write some poems or stories. I told her she could dictate the stories to me, and I would type them for her. She thought this would be fun.

During the following session of 45 minutes, she dictated a story about the Lone Ranger which seemed to be a composite of any number of radio and TV programs. I gave her the typed copy. The following week Karen did not come to the counseling session. After some searching the office personnel located her and sent her to my office. She said that she had forgotten to come. I told her that this was allright but that it was also perfectly allright for her to tell me if she did not wish to come. She insisted that she had just forgotten. Karen went on to say that she did have something which she wished to tell me. She wanted to do something for her "dearest friend, Annie." Karen felt that Annie's heart would be broken if she did not receive a part in the school play. I told Karen that I could not speak for the drama coach but that I would arrange an appointment for her if she wished to speak with him. This I did. Karen then said that she was doing well in her classes and that she had not lost her temper recently. She was spending her extracurricular time with Annie and was avoiding the other children who annoyed her. She thought her teachers were a good group this year, and so far everything was going quite well.

For a number of weeks, I saved the appointed hour for Karen only to have her report that she was too busy and had to use her study hall time. A few times she left braille poems and stories that she had written for me to read, I accepted her failure to use the time without comment although I was beginning to wonder if I were being fair to the other students who might have used this hour.

Karen Uses Her Counselor

One day, about halfway through her scheduled hour, Karen arrived quite unexpectedly. She was shaking, crying, and sobbing. She said that she had come to tell me that she was too busy and upset to write stories. I asked her to sit down, and she poured out the following comments. She just could not go on the way she was. Everything was piling up on her. Her teachers were beginning to scream at her; and, to top it off, her housemother had forbidden her to have anything more to do with Annie. When I asked why this had been done, she said she didn't know. She also said that she somehow managed to get through the week, but she couldn't bear the weekends. Most of the children went home for the weekends, but she never did because her mother was too busy.

Up to this point I had been completely accepting and largely nondirective. I now told Karen that, at times, we all feel like things are piling up and that, perhaps, together we could examine some of her problems. In reference to her statement that all her teachers were turning against her, I asked if it wasn't possible for her to accept the fact that they had their good moods as well as their bad. I explained that I too had bad moods occasionally, and I hoped that she wouldn't feel that I was ever against her. I went on to ask her if she didn't want people to also accept her good and bad moods. Karen completely rejected all of my comments by saying that she always tried to be nice to everyone.

After Karen left my office, I checked into her weekend problem. The staff reported that Karen's mother was too unstable to handle the girls at home and that, unless Karen's father was at home, it was better for Karen to remain at school. I also inquired into Karen's relationship with Annie. The matron told me that school policy did not encourage the girls to form "exclusive" friendships for they felt these relationships led to "trouble." I explained that for Karen this friendship had been quite supportive and pointed out how necessary the relationship was to her. The matron agreed that perhaps a mistake had been made in this particular situation.

The following week, Karen came into my office in high spirits. She was now permitted to associate with Annie. She also reported that she had talked with her father on the telephone and that he was trying to find a job which would keep him at home. She read me a composition on a current popular singer which she had written for English and for which she had received an "A".

As the reports on Karen became increasingly favorable, that is, her teachers and housemother reported that Karen was a changed girl, I considered reducing the number of our counseling sessions. However, I hesitated to do so because of the support which Karen was receiving and, therefore, decided to continue.

Before Thanksgiving vacation Karen came in carrying a dog-eared picture of her favorite singer. She reported that her vacation would not be a happy one as her singer had been killed in an accident. She told me that she was planning her own private burial service for him. She intended to place his pictures, his records, and the poems and letters which she had written to him in a box and bury them.

After Thanksgiving Karen came in and told me that she had been having bad dreams in which she envisioned her singer being hit by a car. She said that the dream kept recurring, and she had terrible pains in her stomach all during vacation. She went on to say that all the girls were teasing her about her singer and calling her crazy. Karen reported that at night she went outside to be alone with her thoughts about her singer. One night she saw a star that was very bright and she feels that this was his star. She also has heard him talk to her. I did not question her stories of her special communion with her singer but listened attentively. Several of Karen's teachers came to me because they were concerned about Karen's preoccupation with the singer's death and have mentioned several explosive crying spells which she has had.

With the exception of typing, Karen's grades at the end of the first report period were quite good. When Karen heard about her typing mark, she burst into a mad raging torrent of words and pounded on the table. She said that she could not put up with her typing teacher and that she could not learn to use the typewriter without using her eyes. I made no attempt to stop her or to comfort Karen. She concluded by saying that Mrs.—— was just like her mother—crabby and not understanding. When she finished, I spoke of how excellent the rest of her report card was. I pointed out to her that good seeing typists do not use their eyes to watch the typewriter. I closed my eyes and showed her how I typed and then asked her to sit down at the typewriter and try. She typed very slowly with her eyes closed and then asked me what she had typed. There were several distorted lines of her singer's name. I explained to Karen that it was important for her to learn the touch system if she wanted to become an efficient typist. I made a copy of the keyboard for her to study.

Counseling has continued in the manner described. I have attempted to work with Karen by being supportive and understanding. We have talked about her dress, which has been atrocious at times, and about her personal health habits. Karen has had some problems in using the Braille system as her eyesight is almost good enough for reading. She is reluctant to learn to use her tactual senses although one day this will be necessary for her eyesight is deteriorating. Counseling will continue with Karen for some time to come.

Discussion

Counseling with Karen has been a frustrating and discouraging experience, and yet it has also been rewarding. I believe that the counselor who can do the most for this type of girl is the one who is willing to be accepting and understanding. Karen was not capable of a great amount of insight and those she will make will come slowly. I did not and do not believe that I should have made an issue out of Karen's fantasy. Karen will have to learn to face reality in a more mature manner, but it is probable that many of her pleasures will by necessity come from an imaginative mind.

I was able to manipulate, to some extent, Karen's environment at the school and felt that this was necessary. Karen needed the friendship of Annie as she needed her fantasy concerning her singer. I realize that the latter could have gotten out of hand but had the feeling at the time that it was serving a useful purpose. I was encouraged to note that Karen's academic record improved considerably and interpreted this as a favorable sign. Also, Karen gradually lengthened the time between emotional outbursts. In short, I believe that Karen's improvement has been a direct result of the three relationships which she experienced, relationships with: Annie, her singer, and myself. Helping her, of course, was the striving found in most individuals towards better self-understanding and maturity.

There is one other point which I would like to raise. Karen was a disturbed girl. Neither by training nor inclination did I feel able to investigate this area. I am sure that there are those who would say that Karen should have been offered psychiatric treatment. This was not possible. Is a counselor treading on dangerous ground by working with a girl such as Karen? Were my procedures correct? How else might I have handled the case?

14...
Everybody's Against Me

Roger was a seven-year-old boy who was in a constant state of warfare with his teachers, his school, and those around him. According to reports from his teachers, he was highly disturbed and prepsychotic. They based their opinion on the following observations. Roger spoke in a high-pitched, strained voice; he stuttered badly at times, talked constantly about his "enemies" at school, and planned devious ways of getting even with them.

Other children made Roger the butt of their jokes and provoked him into doing ridiculous things. As a result of this, he created a constant disturbance in the classroom. He was also very clumsy and failed to participate successfully in any kind of play that involved physical skills. His second grade teacher reported that he rarely completed his school work although she had the impression that he was a bright child. At times she reported that Roger was almost pathetic in his attempt at making a satisfactory impression on his peers by clowning. His efforts in this area invariably failed.

For over two years the school personnel tried to get Roger's parents to recognize the boy's problems and to seek help for his emotional disturbances. During this period there was no trained person within the school who could work with Roger or his parents. Also for some reason the parents and the school never seemed to be able to agree as to what should be done for Roger or who should do it.

This was the situation when I arrived as a counselor in this school. There was no doubt that Roger needed help badly. Also, as Roger was an extremely disrupting influence in the school, one might say that the school was also in need of help.

The Counseling Session

I made an appointment with Roger's parents for an interview. Both parents were reserved and on the defensive during this first interview. However, it soon became apparent that they were quite concerned about the problems of their son. They seemed to recognize that somehow they had failed in their attempts to help Roger. They assured me both by their words and attitudes that they were sincerely interested in helping Roger with his problems. At the time it appeared to me that the major home problem revolved around Roger and his mother. For this reason I asked Roger's mother to come for another interview the following week. The time was such that Roger's father was unable to attend.

"Why do I try so hard and fail so miserably at everything? Now I've failed Roger." These words spoken by Roger's mother during our next meeting gave me the opening I sought. From our prior conversation I had found that Roger's home could be characterized in two ways. First, everyone waited on him hand and foot; and, secondly, there was extreme overprotection. I explained to Roger's mother that the important thing was not her past failure with Roger but that she was now sincerely interested in helping him. I went on to point out that as a youngster grows up he needs to be allowed increasing responsibility for his actions and that protecting him from mistakes and hurt creates an unrealistic sheltered environment that does not prepare him for his future role in an adult world. I told her that, if she wanted to do so, we would arrange to get together for half an hour once a week, and I would work with her on these problems. She most eagerly consented. During the time I was seeing her, I also saw Roger for an equal amount of time.

Most of the first counseling sessions with Roger were spent in my listening to him talk about his enemies and how he would get even with them. I listened sympathetically and neither condemned nor condoned his statements. Gradually he dropped this favorite topic and began to occupy himself with more realistic matters concerning his school, home, and neighborhood.

I was much more directive with Roger's mother. Here I attempted to challenge her assumptions about the boy and to lead her into new concepts about his needs and her own role in helping him. She offered complaints about how hard he was to manage in matters related to dressing, eating, and the like. We began to investigate ways in which his mother could manage him. If Roger was not dressed in time, he could not eat breakfast with his mother and father, a cherished act. If he did not clean up after breakfast, he would not get a coveted ride to school with his father. Roger began to respond favorably immediately. The new routine began to spread to other areas. Roger became more interested in things around him, began to take an interest in schoolwork, and his achievement in all areas improved remarkably.

Discussion

This case and others of a similar nature have forced me to consider to what extent a school counselor should become involved in the personal problems of parents. I believe that I was fortunate that Roger's mother was able to change her behavior. Can I conclude this means that her prior behavior was not dictated by her own personality needs? That is, was it only information that she needed to help her to help Roger? I suppose the fact that she was able to modify her behavior indicates that her problems were not too intense. Or, was it that Roger's behavior became so impossible that it overshadowed her personal problems? What would I have done if Roger's mother had not been able to modify her behavior?

15...
To Hell With My Mother

Lewis came to our university counseling center at the insistence of his mother. Earlier he had dropped out of the university with the statement that he had found it impossible to study. At the time of his withdrawal, he was in the second year of a predental curriculum. The boy had told his parents that he was unable to concentrate on his studies and had withdrawn to avoid failing.

The first contact with the counseling center was made for Lewis by his mother. She made an appointment for Lewis but later called to cancel it since Lewis had decided he did not want counseling. Several weeks after this, Lewis made an appointment and kept it. When he came, he indicated that he had refused to keep the first appointment because he had gone to an agency for counseling when he was a senior in high school and his impression of it was unfavorable. This agency had given him about eight hours of testing, told him that he had the ability to go to college, had suggested that he should enroll in a liberal arts curriculum. His mother had decided that a predental course would be best to follow within this curriculum. "If this is counseling," said Lewis, "I want no more of it."

I explained to Lewis that counseling, as I saw it, did not include my making decisions for him. I further told him that I believed him to be quite capable of making his own decisions, but that, if he wished, I would be glad to listen to him and to help him consider the nature of his problems. Lewis agreed that this was what he wanted.

I asked Lewis to talk about himself and his background in relationship to his study problem. It soon became clear that Lewis did not make his own decisions. For as long as he could remember, his mother had made the decisions for everyone in the family, including his father and his younger brother. She was the driving and dominating force within the family group. No one did anything without mother's consent. Lewis tried to conceal his resentment of his mother, but he was not very successful.

The problem, as Lewis saw it, was what to do with his life. Should he get a job or should he join the army? Or, could he take some tests to discover if there was some other college course he might pursue? I made no comments during this time, for Lewis was verbalizing well and did not seem to be asking questions for which he expected an answer. I also had the impression that there was more to come, that is to say, that Lewis was getting rid of some superfluous verbalizing.

Before I saw Lewis for a second interview, I received a phone call from his mother. She asked if she could come to my office. I granted her an appointment. After a preliminary exchange of conventionalities, Mrs.—— expressed deep concern over the fact that her son had dropped out of college. Mrs.—— felt that a college education was all important and that her son's action was a major tragedy in her life. In addition she expressed a feeling of guilt over the part she might have played in Lewis's predicament. She said that she realized that she had a tendency to be domineering and overprotective but that she did not feel she could help being as she was. She had been under the psychiatric treatment of several therapists with little success. She went on to express concern for her son's emotional well being. Mrs.—— indicated that her husband rejected the notion that Lewis had an emotional problem that could be helped with psychotherapy; his rejection was largely a result of his wife's experiences with therapy. From my conversation with Mrs.——, I got the impression that she was genuinely concerned about her son but that any help Lewis would receive would have to come from himself.

I saw Lewis four times after this conversation with his mother. Lewis requested that he be given interest and aptitude tests. Although I saw no point in giving these tests to Lewis, I did so anyway for Lewis seemed to need a rational reason for coming in to see me. We talked only briefly about the tests and the subject always shifted to the home situation. His hostility and resentment toward his mother became more evident with each session. I began to interpret Lewis's comments in terms of his dependent relationship with his mother and his increasing need for independence.

As the counseling sessions were now in the area of personality dynamics, I suggested to Lewis that some personality testing might be helpful. His projective tests revealed an over-identification with his mother, a hesitance in being self-assertive, and a fear of aggression and of expression of his masculinity. There were also signs of emotional immaturity and conflict in the sexual area. There was an indication of a constant block in achievement caused by too much perfectionism and narcissism. In short, the projective tests substantiated what I had learned from my interviews with him. I interpreted the results to Lewis in relationship to his dependency upon his mother. He seemed to be gaining insight into this problem and talked freely about it.

Lewis came to the fourth session and talked about joining the Army. His mother and friends had belittled the idea. His mother told him that if he joined the Army, he was not to count on any help from her when he returned home. I made no attempt to persuade him or dissuade him. I again told him that he needed to make his own decisions and that I had no advice to give him.

An Explosive Conclusion

The fifth interview turned out to be the last one. Lewis came into my office, leaned over my desk, pounded it with his fist, and said, "To hell with my mother! I've enlisted in the Army and when I leave I don't ever want to see her again!" After he regained his composure, he began to apologize for his outburst. I stopped him with the comment that he need not apologize to me. He had made a decision and the importance of the decision was ample reason for his emotional outburst. I went on to ask him if he realized what this action meant. We continued to talk briefly about his assertion of independence. Lewis recognized that he had made the first step but that he still had a distance to go before he would completely understand himself and would be able to tolerate his mother. The interview concluded on this note.

Discussion

On thinking over the way I handled this case, I have wondered if I took too active a role. Did my direct interpretation of Lewis's comments and projective test results precipitate the final "explosion"? Would a more moderate approach in the sessions have prolonged counseling? Would there have been a more gradual development of insight and a more favorable outcome? At no time during counseling did Lewis reject my interpretations. This indicated to me that his aggression and hostility towards his mother was at, or almost at, the conscious level. Actually, as it turned out, I think Lewis will profit from his Army experience. Being more responsible for himself and living apart from his home environment should give him time to develop his independence and to understand himself better in relationship to his family.

There is another interesting issue which this case raises. In reviewing the data which I have on Lewis, I became convinced that any number of possible theoretical interpretations could have been made. Certainly a Freudian counselor would have seen Oedipal complications; a Rankian would have seen Lewis's need to realize that his mother was not an extension of himself; an Adlerian would have seen the problem as one of attaining a sense of personal significance or superiority in relationship to other people. Frankl, a more recent theorist, would see Lewis as existing in an "existential vacuum."

I do not adhere to any specific personality theory and have many times wondered if a personality theory is not more revealing of the theorist or the holder of the theory than it is of personality. While listening to psychologists and counselors talk and in watching them counsel, I have begun to wonder if the crucial element is not the conviction and sincerity of the counselor rather than the veracity of the counselor's interpretations. In other words, the importance of an interpretation to a counselee may well lie in the realm of whether he *believes* it to be true and not if it *is* true. Indeed, I have a psychologist friend who half seriously propounds a "Do-It-Yourself" counseling technique. In this technique the counselee places his right arm behind his head so that his right hand rests lightly upon his forehead. The counselee talks to himself out loud; and after he raises each problem, he pats himself on the forehead interspersing comments of, "But it's all right, it's all right." This "Do-It-Yourself" theorist maintains that he sometimes thinks that if you could convince the counselee of the efficacy of this technique, its use might be as effective as some of the other techniques which are practiced in counseling.

There is one last point. It will be remembered that I gave Lewis some interest and aptitude tests not because of any conviction that he needed them but because they seemed to give Lewis a reason for coming to the earlier counseling sessions. I am not sure that this use of psychological testing is justifiable. Perhaps psychological testing has been oversold to today's public. I have noticed that some counselees do not feel that they are getting adequate counseling unless they are given a battery of psychological tests. I wonder how a counselor should handle this problem. Are we justified in giving these tests in the circumstances which I have described? Is this an unethical or unwise use of testing?

16...
You Won't Get A Job

Miss Wise, a forty-six-year-old divorcee, was first seen by me six months ago when she applied to the agency for help in seeking employment. In the initial and subsequent visits, she complained bitterly of being rejected for work because she was Jewish and also because she had a breast removed. Miss Wise felt that Jewish employers were the biggest anti-Semites since they employed non-Jewish help and refused to hire her. She also criticized my agency when she discovered that we employed non-Jews.

Several years prior to this time she was referred by a state agency, to which she had gone for employment and medical services and for a psychiatric evaluation. The psychiatrist's diagnosis was that of a severe character neurosis and idiopathic epilepsy, which was controlled without medication. She complained to the psychiatrist about having dizzy spells, difficulty in sleeping, being afraid of cancer, and having an inferiority complex about her excessive weight. After this psychiatric evaluation, Miss Wise dropped out of the picture until about a year later when she came to an outpatient clinic for help because of acute anxiety over her father's death. From this clinic she was referred back to the state agency where she was given another psychiatric evaluation. This time the diagnosis was an anxiety state with paranoid trends. The psychiatrist further stated that Miss Wise was having difficulty with her sexual identification and was extremely dependent. He recommended twenty-five therapy sessions which the state subsequently approved. After twenty visits, he indicated that progress was being made but that she was extremely dependent and demanded a great deal of attention. He mentioned that on three or four occasions he found it necessary to hang up the phone while Miss

Wise was talking since she refused to conclude her conversations. The psychiatrist recommended an additional thirty visits which were approved. During these sessions Miss Wise attended a secretarial school to improve her vocational skills.

Toward the end of Miss Wise's therapy, the psychiatrist indicated that he felt that progress was being made but that her dependency was still a serious problem. He further explained that the patient regarded the treatment as shameful, that she unnecessarily complicated the problem by seeking aid from a considerable number of social agencies within the city, and that when she was frustrated in solving a problem she would defend herself by imagining she was being persecuted. He believed there was evidence that she could accept and understand intellectually but that she could not modify her behavior. The psychiatrist also expressed a fear that Miss Wise would soon accuse him of seeing her only because of the fee involved. Because of this fear and because he felt nothing further could be accomplished in therapy, these sessions were terminated. The psychiatrist's parting comment was that he hoped that the shock of termination might be beneficial.

After this termination Miss Wise returned to the state counselor where she became increasingly hostile in her demand for help in securing employment. The state agency closed her case shortly thereafter when she became so belligerent that it was necessary to have the police remove her from the office. Miss Wise's next stop was in our agency which provides vocational guidance services.

From Our Records

Miss Wise told us that in World War II she had worked for two years as a comptometer operator and one year in a clerical position. Since that time she has held six or seven jobs for no longer than six weeks each. The reason for dismissal from all of these positions was interpersonal difficulties. She has been unemployed for the past four years.

With successful job placement as the ultimate goal, we scheduled weekly counseling sessions with Miss Wise in an attempt to help her obtain more positive interpersonal skills. We reviewed her past history and discussed at length the reasons for her dismissals and the ways in which these difficulties could possibly have been avoided. She appeared to understand but as soon as she felt threatened she would immediately revert to the position that she could not obtain employment because she was Jewish and because her prospective employers resented the fact that one of her breasts had been removed. My attempts to alter this perception through logic were in vain. Her frustration increased as she failed to get a job from the referrals I provided, and she became overtly hostile. She accused my agency of being anti-Semitic because we employ a Negro secretary and then went over the head of our executive director to submit a complaint. The day of this incident she came to my office and stated that the agency was no damn good, that we had not done a thing for her since she had come to us, and that we hated Jews just as much as everyone else.

Becoming angry but not raising my voice much above my normal tone, I told her quite forcibly that she was not required to utilize our services and that if she felt that she was wasting her time she need not bother to come to see me. I further stated that if she would devote more time to selling her skills rather than to attempting to determine who discriminates, she would probably be far more successful. Bluntly I told her that if she would keep her mouth shut about her breast, no one would notice; and then I stated that her biggest problem was that she talked too much about things which had absolutely no relationship to employment. I concluded by saying that if she continued in her behavior she would probably never get a job.

Speechless she left my office crying. I made no attempt to console her. She returned the following week for her appointment, and her behavior was markedly changed. She was quiet and cooperative during the entire session, and she made no reference to being persecuted. Shortly after this meeting, I referred her to a temporary job which she obtained and held successfully for the nine weeks that it lasted. Unfortunately the job has expired, and we have not been able to find other work for her. In spite of this, she has remained cooperative and has kept her hostility under control. Since this incident there have been no outbursts, scenes, or accusations.

Discussion

Although this client was accepted by me from the beginning, her ideas regarding her difficulty in getting a job were never tolerated. Or perhaps I should say I never verbally agreed with her and tried to point out that some of her accusations were illogical. The interesting factor is that I made no apparent headway until I became almost overtly aggressive in my attitude toward her behavior. I can't help but wonder if I did the right thing even though this action seems to have had desirable results. I wonder what the final outcome of this case will be. Is it better for this woman to express herself in an undesirable way and as a result remain unemployable or would it be better for her to control her behavior and not be able to vent her hostilities? Apparently she has not gained insight either as a function of psychiatric therapy or my counseling. Will this have a dire effect at some time in the future? How else could I have handled this woman? Did I help her? Are there some individuals who cannot he helped? I had the feeling that this woman desperately wanted aid. This is evidenced by her visits to numerous agencies and in her conversations with me. However, I have the feeling that this woman does not understand herself any better today than she did before psychiatric therapy and vocational counseling were initiated. Another point that has bothered me is whether a vocational counselor should attempt to place a person such as this. What is my responsibility to the employer? Also, I am extremely curious about the change in this woman's behavior. What actually caused Miss Wise to modify her actions? How lasting will this change be? There is another issue here which is a major one. Undoubtedly this woman is at best a psychoneurotic and possibly verges on being a psychotic. I would have been more comfortable if I had not taken this case for I do not believe it was within the vocational guidance domain. On the other hand, she had profited minimally from therapy, if at all, would not be referred for further therapy, and did need help. Are there exceptions which counselors should make when a counselee needs help but cannot or will not go elsewhere? I confess I do not know the answer to this question and am not certain that my actions were correct.

17...

They All Kick You
When You're Down

Mary, a thirty-five-year-old woman, was referred to our vocational guidance and placement agency by a social worker. Mary had been recently released on an indefinite "home-visit" status from a state mental hospital. There she had been diagnosed and treated for paranoid schizophrenia. The hospital report indicated that her state was believed to be fairly satisfactory but that her employment should involve limited responsibility.

I found Mary to be somewhat withdrawn and suspicious. Her personal appearance was ragged and untidy, and she had a pallor which I assumed was a result of being institutionalized. Mary was employed as a counter girl, on a part time basis, in a restaurant owned by a relative. The job had been given her to expedite her release from the hospital. She expressed a dislike for restaurant work and stated a preference to return to the secretarial field where she had previously worked. She had made an unsuccessful attempt to regain her position as a secretary to an executive in a local manufacturing business.

Prior to Mary's hospitalization, her marriage of eight years standing had disintegrated to the point of separation. After her release from the hospital, she had attempted a reconciliation with her husband; but he had rejected her attempts and had initiated divorce proceedings. He would not permit her to visit with their four-year-old child.

I learned from Mary's former employer that she had developed an extremely dependent relationship with him and that he felt her behavior had bordered on seductiveness. Even after Mary learned that she would not be considered for re-employment, she had continued to call and make such a nuisance of herself that the firm threatened her with police action. It seemed to me that these two rejections were instrumental in the creation of Mary's present problem. She had withdrawn and had become less responsive. Her grasp on reality now appeared to be on tenuous grounds. In spite of this, I had the feeling that Mary could be helped to help herself. I should add that during this period Mary was reporting regularly to the hospital outpatient clinic for psychiatric consultation and medication.

In my earliest counseling sessions with Mary, I attempted to motivate her to improve her appearance and to become more active in her search for employment. I reviewed her employment history with her pointing out that it was excellent and that she had many marketable skills. After discussing the type of jobs she might be both interested in and suited for, Mary decided that she would pursue positions which would utilize her office skills but would not involve the responsibilities of a secretarial position. After Mary decided this, I referred her to many job openings which were closely related to what she desired. She reported that she was unsuccessful in obtaining any of these positions. We began to analyze this lack of success. Mary stated that she believed that her hospitalization was a stigma against her and because her former employer would not accept her, no one would accept her. Her descriptions of her employment interviews revealed that she had acted in an extremely hostile manner toward the interviewers.

A Crucial Session

Soon after this interview, I received a call from Mary's social worker who reported that Mary was making little effort to find work. She had been sleeping late and had missed several days at her part time job. In addition she had not followed through on several job referrals. As a result of this conversation, I called several employers and learned that Mary's personal appearance had been atrocious at the interview. She had, in fact, gone to one interview with curlers in her hair. Most of the employers felt that she did not want the job. They reported that she was aggressive and hostile towards them.

Mary came for her fourteenth counseling session. She again mentioned the supposed stigma of hospitalization. I asked her if she had really made an effort to obtain employment. In an indignant manner she stated that she had done everything possible. As she talked, she raised her voice to complain that no one would even look at her.

At this point I confronted her with the information I had obtained. She reacted in a non-committal manner. I then suggested that as she had been rejected by her former employer and her husband, she was afraid it would happen again and consequently acted in a manner which made her employment impossible. She vehemently denied my statement, said that no one would give her a chance, and concluded by shouting, "They all kick you when you're down!"

My reaction was immediate and as extreme as hers. I told her that I did not intend to spend my time playing games with her; and, although she had come to me for help in finding a job, she now was spending her time wallowing in self-pity. I went on to say that she had made no attempt to help herself or accept any help which I might be able to offer. Furthermore, I asked her how could she expect to find work if she spent half of her day in bed and did not follow through on job referrals. Did she expect an employer to help her when she arrived at an interview looking like she had just been in a tornado or when she verbally abused him? Did she think that if she were the employer that she would hire a person such as herself? Her reaction to my questions was one of passive amazement. She did not comment but appeared dumbfounded.

At this point I lowered my voice and told Mary that I sincerely wanted to help her; but because of her present attitude and behavior I did not know whether she wanted help at this time. I further stated that I did not feel that anything more could be gained by continuing counseling under the existing conditions since she was not being honest and was not cooperating. I terminated the interview by suggesting to Mary that she give some thought to our conversation and that if she felt that something further could be accomplished she should contact me.

About one week later Mary came to my office without an appointment. When she stepped into my office, I was most pleasantly surprised. No longer did I see a drab, sloppy individual, but an attractive, well-groomed woman. She initiated the interview by stating that after giving my comments considerable thought, she had realized that I had been justified in talking as I did to her and that she had been behaving like a "two-year-old." She further astonished me by adding that she had found a job as a clerk stenographer which she was to begin the following day.

I brought up the question of the possibility of further counseling to which she readily agreed. Counseling was terminated after four more sessions at which point we both felt that she was adequately prepared to accept the stresses and responsibilities of her job. From the comments of the social worker, I have learned that Mary continues to work for the same concern and recently has been promoted to a more responsible position.

Discussion

I must admit that this case intrigues and amazes me. I have analyzed the situation in the following manner. Apparently Mary had profited from her institutionalization but had then become caught in a vicious circle of self-pity and defeatism. My reaction to her in the fourteenth counseling session was a spontaneous, honest, and luckily accurate appraisal of the situation. The intensity of my reaction literally dynamited Mary out of her dilemma. In retrospect I have also realized that a major part of my reaction was due to my feelings that I had been "taken in" by Mary. That is to say, my professional pride was offended. As a result of this incident, I think I also have grown. I believe that for Mary a crucial part of my reaction involved not only the shock of my words but also the realization that it was her behavior to which I was reacting. In other words, I did not reject her; I rejected only her behavior. Her past experiences with males had involved a rejection of both her *and* her behavior. The two factors had become, therefore, one in her mind. Mary reinforced this analysis when, in our last session, she told me that she could now understand that her relationship with her former employer had been inappropriate. She could now also see that he was justified in not re-employing her.

I would hesitate to recommend my procedure to another counselor. I believe that it was successful in part because it was an honest reaction. I do not believe that it would have been successful if I had manufactured my emotions as a calculated move. Furthermore, I can see how, if Mary had not been able to cope with the situation, I might have done actual harm.

18...

Fighting For Adjustment

Frank came to our center; the final rung in an extensive referral ladder. His initial offense had been the theft of a bicycle. This started a sequence of events which took him through as complicated a medical, psychiatric, psychological, and sociological evaluation as I have ever seen. I shall not attempt to report the detailed findings from these evaluations except to note that Frank, medically and psychologically, was checked on everything from syphilis to sanity. Medically, Frank is a healthy, fifteen-year-old boy. Intellectually, he is a low-normal individual. Emotionally he is a seriously disturbed person.

In order to understand Frank, his home environment must be considered. Frank is the youngest of five boys and older than three sisters. His father is employed as a truck driver, has worked steadily, and, apparently has been able to provide the basic necessities for his family.

From the records of the board of education, we found that Frank began to get into difficulty as soon as he entered school. He needed constant supervision, was a disrupting influence, and, in general, showed little interest in his work. From the fourth grade on, Frank's behavior began to effect other community agencies. Petty theft, minor vandalisms, and other problems checkered his early years.

Frank's mother states that he has always felt that his parents loved his brothers and sisters more than they did him. She further states that his lies, thefts, and fights have reached the place where she is no longer capable of handling him or influencing him. Prior to the culminating incident, she had filed a delinquency petition with the court charging that Frank had become too difficult to handle at home.

At one time the family had placed him with a brother in the hope that the influence of the brother and the change in environment would be of some assistance to Frank. Soon afterwards the brother sent Frank home because of the boy's impossible behavior.

The caseworker reported that his impression of Frank's mother was that she was an emotionally deprived individual. She was unable to express her own repressed feelings and, therefore, would not tolerate the expression of her children's feelings. Furthermore, Frank's mother held high standards for herself and consequently expected almost perfect behavior from her children. The caseworker also had the impression that she had gradually come to focus all of her self-dissatisfaction and the family's poor living conditions upon Frank. Frank's father was seen as an ineffectual man who works hard and wants nothing else except to be left in peace.

Conduct of the Case

It was decided that both Frank and his mother would be amenable for group counseling. Frank was placed in a group of ten boys who were between the ages of fifteen and seventeen. All of them had been adjudged delinquents by the Municipal Court and placed on probation. The boys were first offenders and were not considered to be habitual delinquents. They were also all of low-normal intelligence and came from about the same socio-economic background. Frank's mother was placed in a group which was composed of the parents of these same boys.

When the group sessions began, Frank was extremely hostile. He was unable to concentrate or to remain quiet for any lengthy period of time. He expressed open hostility towards all forms of authority: parental, judicial, or educational. Frank rejected the friendship of the group members and was a definite source of agitation within the group. He would withdraw almost completely when "attacked" by a group member for disrupting the continuity of the group. Although he was continually censured by other members, Frank's behavior continued for several months.

The turning point for Frank occurred one day as he was going home from school. He saw one of his group members attacked by a gang of boys. After giving the matter some thought, Frank joined the fray and rescued the group member. The next day this incident was related to the group. The group immediately began to accept Frank as an integral part of their intellectual and social community. Frank had finally found the stature and the acceptance which he had so desperately needed.

After this there was a decided change in Frank's behavior. He no longer resorted to infantile behavior to gain attention. His belligerency and hostility continued to decrease. Along with this change in behavior, his understanding of his home situation increased, and he began to make definite attempts to improve his relationship with his parents.

Of course, it is too soon to know what sort of an adult Frank will make. My guess would be that his understanding of himself will continue to grow and that one day he will take an acceptable place in society.

While Frank was undergoing group counseling, his mother was a part of a parental group. In the early sessions she continually talked about the "terrible behavior" of her son. After listening to the other group members and discussing her problems with them, she began to gain insight into her own problems. She started to realize that her son had certain positive features. That, as one group member put it, "He couldn't be as bad as she thought." She realized that she had been expecting too much of Frank and had not given him credit for his accomplishments. She developed a more understanding attitude and made plans to re-evaluate her feelings toward the boy. These group sessions were the only "social outlets" which she had, and she often expressed gratitude for being selected as a member of the group. It is the impression of the counselor that she is no longer as depressed as she once was. She has "grown" considerably and has become a more relaxed individual.

Discussion

I have some definite opinions on the use of group counseling. It most definitely is not the panacea of the overworked counselor. It is a technique and when properly used a very good technique. There are situations where I do not believe it should be used. For example, I do not believe it should be used where the group members know each other socially. Personal feelings and experiences are frequently expressed; and, unfortunately, human nature being what it is, these experiences are likely to be taken out of the counseling session and to become the subjects of a gossiping session. If the intimate matters discussed in the group session become public domain, then the insights gained could be completely destroyed. This would mean that group counseling of a personal nature should not be used in the school setting where all the children know each other, nor should it be used in the community where the group members socialize with each other.

Group counseling is most productive when the members of the group have much in common. It should be noted that this was true for both Frank and his mother. The insights of group members seem to be facilitated when the group can discuss common problem areas and when the members tend to resemble each other both intellectually and emotionally.

19...

No Desire To Live

Irene, a thirteen-year-old girl in the ninth grade, first came to my attention when a municipal agency called my office. Irene had attempted to commit suicide by drinking iodine and was being held for study prior to a court hearing. At the court hearing Irene was placed on probation with the stipulation that she be given psychiatric treatment. I was asked to prepare a report for the agency where Irene was to be given this treatment.

In going over the school records, it became apparent that several serious mistakes had been made. Irene, who had entered our school three months previously, had been placed in a class for children with below normal intelligence. Records from her previous school revealed that Irene had not only skipped two grades but also had been on the honor roll. Irene's failing grades in all of her present subjects had kept this error from being noticed. Further, our principal and teachers had been severely critical of the girl because of minor insubordination in class. When I advised the principal of the incorrect placement, he became immediately concerned and agreed that when Irene returned to school some remedial action would be taken.

To better understand Irene, I contacted several agencies and gained the following information. Irene was the second child in a family of four children. Her father, a chronic alcoholic, had deserted the family about six months prior to Irene's suicide attempt. Her mother was a "rigid punitive woman" who had little warmth or affection for any of her children and was overtly hostile toward Irene. She had an older brother sixteen years old and two younger sisters who were twelve and ten. The family had been living on a grant from the Department of Public Assistance since Irene's birth.

I contacted the probation office and found that the girl explained her suicide attempt to the court by saying that she had attempted to take her life because of the guilt she felt about having had sexual intercourse with two boys the previous month. The diagnostic examination, given at the Court's request, revealed that Irene's intelligence was within the normal range (Wechsler Full Scale I.Q. of 110). The examining psychologist had expressed the opinion that Irene had been seriously disturbed when she took the test; and, consequently, this score should be considered as being at the lower limit of her measurable intellectual capacity. The psychiatrist described Irene as being hyperactive during his interview. He reported that the girl had had continued nightmares over several years and diagnosed her disturbance as a conduct disorder with neurotic traits. As the court had referred Irene to a clinic for treatment, I contacted the clinic counselor. At his suggestion I agreed to focus my attention upon helping Irene make a satisfactory school adjustment. The focus of the clinic was to be on Irene's personal problems and her family situation.

School Counseling

When Irene returned to school, she was sent to my office. She was overtly disturbed which was manifested in nail biting and a slight stutter. Irene was sullen and suspicious towards me but was surprised and pleased to learn that I had sent for her because we had discovered her incorrect class placement. We talked of her school problems at some length. She spontaneously told me that one of her main troubles was that she hated the school. She had transferred to the school shortly after her father had deserted the family. Her mother had forced her to make the transfer because she felt that they could no longer afford carfare to the other school. "In this school," said Irene, "no one is interested in me, and I hate everyone." I continued to listen to her as she went on to say that her classmates were "dopes", the work was too easy, and she was bored all the time, and she couldn't be bothered with those "stupid assignments." I told Irene that the school was very sorry about her incorrect placement and that I could well understand how she felt. I agreed with her that being placed with young people whom she did not know and being forced to do work in which she was not interested must have been very discouraging. I asked her if she would like to be placed in a different section. We discussed courses which Irene might take; and I asked her to think about them, discuss them with her mother, and come back the next day with her decision. I told Irene that, in the meantime, I would talk with the principal and her teachers to see what might be done. Irene seemed amazed and thankful for my interest in her.

The next morning Irene returned to my office and said that she would like to transfer to the Academic Course. She said that her mother didn't care what course she took. After a conference with the principal, Irene was placed in a class with children who were at her own ability level. I again assured her that we wished to do everything we could to help her make the necessary adjustments; but I also impressed upon her that she herself would have to assume a large measure of responsibility for her progress. Again, Irene showed a positive response to my offer of assistance and assured me that she would do better in her new class.

Irene seemed reluctant to discuss herself or her home situation, and I did not press her to talk about this area. As I did feel that she needed support in making her new adjustments, I suggested that she come every other week and tell me how she was doing. I also told her to feel free to come in between times if she felt that I could help her. Finally, I told her that I would keep in contact with her teachers to see how she was progressing in her new course of study.

I shared the background information which I had with the principal and Irene's teachers and enlisted their aid in making a real effort to give Irene the special attention and recognition which she needed. At the same time, I stressed to them the need of making Irene aware of her responsibilities and the necessity that they be firm in their demands that Irene measure up to her capabilities.

Until she left the school in June, Irene came in regularly to see me. Her grades improved considerably, and she was able to graduate with her class. She was appreciative of the help she had been given and was grateful to the school for making her life more "bearable." In our counseling sessions, she spoke about her treatment at the clinic. I told her that I had been in touch with the clinic counselor and that both of us would continue to try to help her in any way possible.

The clinic counselor informed me that Irene kept her appointments regularly and that they spent most of the time in their sessions together discussing her problems with her siblings and her parents. In these therapy sessions, she was helped to overcome her feelings of guilt and, with the aid of her counselor, was able to seek more acceptable social satisfactions. The counselor had referred her to a pre-adolescent group in the community, and Irene appeared to gain considerable pleasure from her association with them. Her relationships with boys her own age began to follow the usual adolescent pattern. She stopped biting her nails, was no longer troubled by nightmares, and her stuttering diminished considerably. Her mother refused to have regular contacts with the clinic counselor and refused to see me, the school counselor. I had attempted to get to know Irene's mother by making a home visit only to find myself quite unwelcome. However, as Irene's behavior improved, her mother's pressures on the girl relaxed considerably.

Discussion

In Irene's life her previous school had probably been her chief source of satisfaction and security. Her father's desertion, followed by a shift to a new and unwanted school, plus her mother's increased hostility, stripped Irene of the last remnant of security and status. I believe that her desperation, caused by these factors, precipitated her sexual activities. This, in turn, caused deep guilt feelings which were overwhelming in conjunction with everything else. The depth of Irene's despair can be found in her attempt at suicide. It is tragic that she had no one to whom she could turn.

The school, although inadvertently, must share in the responsibility for intensifying this girl's plight. I believe that one main reason why all of us, her teachers and the principal, united to help this girl was because we felt guilty about a situation which we might have been instrumental in causing.

Irene's case has caused me to reexamine myself as a counselor. I have found that, almost unknowingly, I have been withholding myself from becoming too involved with my counselees. I don't believe that I have been a bad counselor, but somehow Irene has taught me that I must care for my counselees more than I have in the past.

Irene has also caused me to reexamine my attitude towards our school personnel. I had been, and to a degree still am, convinced that a counselor needs to be very careful about the information which he transmits to other school personnel. However, with Irene I felt that it was imperative that the school know what we had done to her and the drastic results so that we could correct our mistakes and help her. I was amazed at the sincere interest and cooperation which I received. I did, of course, stress to them the confidential nature of the information which they were receiving. As far as I know, it has been kept that way by Irene's teachers and principal. Perhaps counselors should always make more of an effort to develop this type of relationship with the school staff.

Finally, I was delighted at the working relationship which developed between myself and the outside agency. We kept in contact with each other and shared discussions of our experiences with Irene. Knowing that Irene was receiving help with her personal problems kept me from feeling that I should attempt to counsel in this area. Although Irene was free to talk about her personal problems if she wished to do so, it was evident that her need was being met elsewhere. One last comment: I must add that, although Irene will never know this, I am certain she helped me as much as a counselor as I helped her as a counselee.

20...
What Should I Be?

Ken was a twenty-eight-year-old veteran of the Korean War. He saw active combat duty and was honorably discharged from the Army. Ken was married but had no children. He came to our agency with the stated purpose of seeking vocational assistance. The vocational counselor, after administering a battery of psychological tests and talking with Ken, decided that there were personal problems in Ken's life that needed consideration in conjunction with Ken's desire for vocational guidance. Ken agreed with this decision and was referred to me, a counseling psychologist.

The interaction of personal problems with vocational decisions occurs quite frequently in counseling. As this interaction was revealed quite clearly in the first counseling session and as several other problems were touched upon, a verbatim report from the tape recording of the first session is given. Ken's case is still in progress so the ultimate outcome can not be given at this time.

The First Counseling Session

K: I know that the chances for Negroes are very slim, and I want to get into something that will be a benefit to me and a credit to my race. I'm not much of a classroom boy, and I want to know what . . . what steps to take to prepare myself. I mean I've done some of everything and of course everywhere I go people think I'm intelligent but on the contrary I'm not. In other words I seem to master anything I undertake as far as a job is concerned. I worked for the Board of Education. I worked for the Navy Procurement Department of Medicine, and the only way I could get in there was to say I had a college education. They couldn't tell any different by my work. That was in California. So I just decided there, right then and there, that in order to make any success in life, I would have to have a little more education. So I struck out to finish high school. My father's a minister, and I've been in the ministry for quite a few years. I've seen so much illiteracy in Negro churches until . . . if I can't be a good minister I don't want to be one at all. And yet I don't want to spend my life under the foot of somebody.

C: You feel then that your interest in preparing yourself for some type of occupation should offer you plenty of security as well as occupational satisfaction.

K: I've looked into almost every phase of mechanical work. In fact I took a test, before I went into service, to be a trainee mechanic. They used to give them down at city hall during the war. And I only made 68 while 70 was passing. I tried all these other tests —different wheels—how they turn and so forth. I didn't make out so good. Everything I undertake around the house mechanically, you know, like carving things turns out poorly. Drawing, I'm messy with that. I don't do much of anything well.

C: You feel that what ability you do have does not lie in the mechanical field.

K: I'm certain of it. Anything clerical . . . if I'm shown or told what to do, is alright. I follow good directions. I have recommendations from everywhere I work. And down here at the factory where I work . . . In fact they hired four fellows, six fellows, and I was the only colored one, and they fired the rest of the boys and kept me on. Gave me a raise. I mean they treat me there just as if I'm one of them. I've had some trouble, but that was due to some form or other I made a mess of.

C: In other words you feel that there you are showing a reasonable degree of success on the job that you have now.

K: Yes, but that's so meager. I mean it's nothing to base any future progress on. I mean I'm just there, and it's not anything stable. I mean I'd probably be there the rest of my life at $1.25 an hour.

C: In other words you're using that as a means to an end.

K: Certainly, that's all it is. I don't know when they'll say, "I can't use you any more," or when their business will go down. I'd like to have some type of profession to fall back on. I think a man living in the world from hand to mouth, from one job to another, and no specialty either, I can't see where it's sensible.

C: In other words you feel that a man must be fully prepared to handle a job that's really worthwhile.

K: Absolutely. Well, that's about all of it in a nutshell. I . . . I'm not able to . . . I mean I don't fear any problem; but unless it's actually worked out plain for me, why I . . . I'm not able to match it, it seems. Now for instance in mathematics, in geometry I mean, I know the stuff when I'm reading it, when doing it. I understand; but when it comes to a matter of tests and I see the exact same thing there, why it's all Greek to me.

C: You feel that you can do something after having been shown, but you have trouble working things out on your own.

K: That's right. Uh . . . and I think mainly that comes from not being able to concentrate. I . . . I can read, understand what I'm reading, and explain what I'm reading but during that course of time my mind will wander off on something that's not altogether what I'm reading about. And I seem to have a . . . what do you call it . . . it's not an obsession but it seems like everything I undertake to do, why it's like I've had a vision of that thing. It's just working out according to something I've dreamed about. And sometimes I wonder, now what did I dream then. And I just go along from day to day like that. If I cross the street and meet a person I've never seen before, some way or another, I dreamed about that person, meeting, occasion, or what not. This fellow said according to my tests, it showed some form of a maladjustment. I know I do have an inferiority complex. I'm certain of that, especially if I'm around white people. And if I'm around fairly intelligent colored people, I don't feel myself a part of that set. I think that at any moment I am going to make an error.

C: In other words you feel that you shy away from people or groups where you think you may not be able to measure up to them.

K: And yet, I like that type of person. I mean I won't mix with any other type of person. I'd rather stay to myself than mix with any common class, that is, unless a person showed me a very satisfactory way of carrying himself according to my beliefs.

C: In other words you do like to be around people with better training; and when you find yourself uncomfortable in their presence, you have a tendency to withdraw and go off by yourself rather than be with those you do not feel measure up to your standards. Is that right?

K: That's right. Uh . . . I don't know . . . I don't feel myself biggity or anything; but even now, we don't have any . . . my wife and I, we're not very sociable; and, as a rule, we live a life to ourselves. And I have appreciated that type of living until lately. And it . . . in my line of work you've got to be sociable, whether in the ministry or any public profession. You can't sit off here by yourself and expect people of your church to think too much of you.

C: In other words you feel that you have more or less been satisfied with this type of existence, but now you realize that you can't be by yourself. You must, in a society, become part of that society in order to have a satisfactory adjustment.

K: That's right. And another thing that's been worrying me is my wife. Uh . . . she's a Methodist, and I'm a Baptist. I guess it was this morning I spoke to her about deciding to become a member of my church because I felt it was essential that she be part of whatever I was a part of. Well, in turn she suggested, "Well, why don't you be a member of my church?" I mean that conflict goes on. Neither one of us will break down, and I feel that being the man of the house, the support of the woman—she don't work, won't work, and she's had a fairly good education—I feel that she should come over to my side. After all she has nothing to lose. I'm the one to make the living for her. I'm the one to be satisfied in whatever step in life I take. And I'm not satisfying her with making a living for her. So long as it's honest. Of course if I was doing something that was dishonest, I'd hesitate to feel that she should agree with me. But within and . . . within any honest range, I feel she should readily agree.

C: In other words it's . . . You're not able to accept her point of view. That is, that there's just as good a reason for you to come over to her faith as for her to come over to yours, and you prefer and have requested that she become a member of your faith.

K: Yes. But of course she is a little high strung. She came up in the Methodist church. Her father was a Methodist minister. She has the idea that the average Baptist is . . . well so ignorant that she don't want to be a part of it. Well, I tried to carry her through the better Baptist churches, and I'd go with her to her churches. In fact, I do like some of the Methodist churches, but I can't stand being bossed around. And of course she holds to the point that if I'd come over to her side, she'd be perfectly happy. And I don't see just, I mean, I'm confused about what step to take. Now I don't know whether I can get over that my scholastical tests here were way below the standard, much below. Yet he said I had an I.Q. of 116 which he couldn't understand.

C: As I get it, you feel that the happiness in your home depends upon, or is with regard to, the faith which you or your wife hold. You feel that both of you should become members of the same faith.

K: I do.

C: And you are wondering why it is that with an I.Q. of 116 you do not show college aptitude.

K: That's right. Up until recently I felt that English was my worst subject but now I . . . English is rather . . . I grasp it very easily, and math and languages are the essential holdbacks. And from what I understand I have to have . . . be able to master those subjects in order to go to college. You know . . . No doubt about it. I'm taking Spanish now, and I'm just breezing through it, getting by, and I don't understand how.

C: You feel you do recognize and accept your shortcomings in being able to master these particular subjects.

K: Yes. And yet I don't know. Maybe my ideals are too high, much beyond my ability. I've been told that before but wouldn't accept it. I mean I'm just not going to say, "Well, I'll give up," and go get a job somewhere . . . forget about it.

C: You feel that you might be trying to accomplish something above the level of your ability, but you're not going to accept the fact that you can't do it.

K: That's right. I feel that if anybody else has done it and made a success of it, I don't know why I can't. Because after all . . . I have been able to fool the public, but I haven't fooled myself. And I'm tired of fooling the public. I'm afraid that sooner or later somebody is going to find out.

C: In other words you feel that eventually you're going to have to admit to yourself the limitations of your ability.

K: Yeah. That's right.

C: Accept them for what they are.

K: That's right. And I don't know what they are. I don't know what I'm suited for. I've read a psychiatry book on choosing a vocation or profession in life, and it said to line up certain professions and certain vocations and to check those you're the most interested in, those you have the least interest in and so forth.

C: Uh-huh.

K: And by doing that you find what procedures to take. Why even that hasn't worked out.

C: Nothing seems to have helped so far.

K: No. Yet, I have the determination. I have the ambition and that's about all.

C: You don't feel that that is enough to make you become successful in what you want to do.

K: No, I don't. The whole thing is a big problem. In fact I want to be something in life, and my wife wants me to be somebody. I'm not . . . just can't give up. That's all there is to it. I have too much at stake. And yet, I'm getting older every day, and whatever I'm going to do I'd better hurry and do it.

C: In other words you feel that you have definitely in mind what you want to do, and you realize that the time for you to get started on it is getting very short, but you're wondering if you really have the ability to carry through on what you want.

K: That's right. I don't know why the situation is working out like this. I mean I . . . don't know. I hardly know what to say about it. All I know is that dissatisfaction is worrisome when you want to be something, and you see you can't.

C: In other words it's pretty hard to accept defeat in yourself.

K: Yes it is. I can't . . . I mean I can't bear the thought of not being something of credit . . . I mean to get out there and to . . . to just work commonly like any other ordinary man. I'm not satisfied with it, and it becomes boring. I change from one job to another. I can't go on through life like that. Other people can do it and be satisfied: go get a job somewhere from somebody, stay there for years, die there . . . but I can't do it. I can look at the progress of other men who haven't had the opportunity that I have had, and they made themselves a credit, and I have the opportunity, and, seemingly, I'm doing nothing with it.

C: You rather hate to feel that others whom you know have made the grade with less help, and you are unable to make the grade with all the help that you can get.

K: That's right. With any progress I could eventually, I probably could, but time is my essential objective now.

C: You feel that what you do is going to have to be decided quickly.

K: Couple of more months and I'll be out of this high school game, this accelerated course, and then . . . in fact, my application should be in now . . . if I'm going to college, or whatever I'm going to do should be decided very soon. It's no use kidding yourself if . . . I'd rather not go to college than be thrown out. I'd just rather get into something that's going to be a benefit. After all that's what I'm looking for. I know nobody can make up your mind for you. I know that, but I do feel that some person's ideas would be able to assist you in helping you to make up your own mind. I mean if a person has no determination to make any progress in life regardless of all the opportunities, advice and what not, he can't make anything out of himself. I've seen that so many times. But I know I do have the ambition, courage to go through with it, if I could get into something that would claim my attention.

C: You feel that it is rather difficult to accept the fact that you may not have the ability to be successful.

K: Yeah. If . . . uh . . . I don't know . . . what to, uh . . . what good these tests are really if they don't help a person in some manner. I mean just to take an aptitude test to tell you . . . show what your I.Q. is, what you're weak in—what you're not weak in —I mean I don't see where that's too much help. Because frankly I . . . If they want to help you and if they can help you, if there is any such thing as being able to help you . . . uh . . . I think in that test they should be able to do so.

C: You feel that the tests should give you more information about yourself and plan in detail just what you should prepare for.

K: Yeah. This fellow said, in fact, that he wouldn't make any definite conclusions on this, and he would report it to someone who was . . . more capable in handling such cases. And that they would be able to give me an idea, at least, of whatever it was that was hindering me, or just what I should do.

C: In other words, the vocational adviser felt that by working through this in the counseling situation, you may better be able to understand and accept yourself for what you are.

K: That's right. I do too. Uh . . . personally I know my ability. I mean I know my own condition but the thing about it is that I want somebody else who's been trained in that type of work—able to help a person along these lines.

C: You feel that you know your limitations, but you want someone else to tell you so.

K: Yes. Because I can't see where I could make progress in one line of work and still have the ambition. I don't see where the two go together. I mean I know there is something that's hindering me, something that's standing in the way. If there wasn't, I'd have given up long ago. If a person finds out definitely he can't do a thing, why he'll gradually lose interest. Well, I haven't lost interest and probably never will.

C: In other words you feel that your progress is being blocked by something other than your ability to do the work.

K: Yes. Well, whether it's the way of study or the type of training I'm getting, I notice if anything is simplified for me, step by step, I can get it easier and not have to depend on my age and what I should know at that age. I had an English teacher who was of that nature, and I changed her and got a woman who was able to start right from rock bottom and teach me how to check on adverbs and what not. And I was able to catch right on. Whereas, my old teacher said, "You know what an adverb is," and so on and so on. Well, I couldn't get it like that.

C: You felt she was assuming too much.

K: Yes. I am wondering if that isn't the case with my mathematical adjustment. I've even . . . I know the classes are pretty well crowded, and they can't give too much individual help to one person. And just to be puzzled with something and to go up and ask why this is and they explain it to you doesn't necessarily determine your understanding of the entire problem, and you're just going around in circles. If you can't understand the whole step, the entire sequence, why then you can't get it. I went to night school just to sit in on a class. I suggested that. And I was able to get more, but I don't see the . . . the idea of going to school in the day and money being spent for that daytime class, and spending the hours and whatnot there, and still not getting what you want, and having to go somewhere at night to try to grasp it.

C: You feel that you're not making satisfactory progress in your work. You're wondering if it's just a waste of time.

K: Yeah. And I'm wondering if you would be able to help me straighten that out. I mean you said you don't give advice, but that's what I want.

C: In other words you feel that you would like to have the whole program laid out for you.

K: Yeah. And if you'd be frank and just tell me what I'm suited for. What . . . is your idea of what thing I'd be successful in?

C: You feel that possibly through working through this thing in a counseling situation that you might get more help and see the answer for yourself.

K: Yeah. I do. And I do always. I think I know definitely if you can explain your problem to another person, they're more able to give you more of a concrete idea. There can't be anything partial in giving that decision. Whereas, myself probably, I wouldn't admit to it. But if somebody would tell me definitely, "I think you're wasting your time here. You'd better just go out and get yourself a job. Your ideals are too high for what you're fitted for." Probably I'd be more willing to accept that as a defeat than saying the same thing to myself.

C: In other words you feel that you find it rather difficult to accept what you really feel yourself, and you prefer having someone else tell you what your limitations are.

K: Yes. Not only telling me what my limitations are but telling me what to do about it.

C: I see that our time is about up for today.

K: All right.

C: Would you like to continue this?

K: Yes, I would if you think you can help me.

C: When do you feel you would like to come in again?

K: Suppose we make it one day next week when you . . . you will go over this.

C: Yes. I'll get the appointment book, and we'll make a definite date.

Discussion

As can be seen in this case, vocational decisions are frequently confused because of personal problems. Ken is questioning his worth as an individual because of his high aspirations and low achievement, because of his racial identification, and because of his marital problems. All of these problems are combining to make a vocational decision very difficult. It is interesting to note how Ken makes the transition of being inadequately accepted in his home to the psychological testing which is interpreted in the same manner.

One of the values of recording an interview is that the counselor can see where he has made mistakes in the interpretation or reflection of a counselee's statements. Note that toward the end of the interview I have not reacted to the content of what Ken is saying. His desire for advice and help is not fully recognized. This would have been an ideal time for me, as a counselor, to restate my confidence that Ken did have the ability to solve his own problems, that through discussing them with me he would be able to make his own decisions. Also, the recording of an interview permits the counselor to check his own verbalistic habits and mannerisms. The phrase "in other words" has been used too frequently in my reflections of Ken's statements.

The phenomenon described by Ken, in which he feels he has met a person before or been someplace at a prior time, is commonly called *déjà vu*. It is a phenomenon which occurs when an individual, upon perceiving something which he has never seen before, has the impression that he has had the experience in the past. In some cases it can be explained by there being a similarity between the present event and some event in the past. It is not uncommon among psychiatric patients but also occurs in normal individuals. In any case the vocational counselor was clearly out of bounds in interpreting this to Ken as a sign of maladjustment, regardless of the truth of the statement. It should be remembered that counselees are prone to interpret a counselor's statements in the light of their personality needs. Counselors should be quite sure that their statements are helping their counselees and not creating additional anxieties.

21...
How Far
Should I Go?

Miss Dha, after seven months in a large coed city college, telephoned for an appointment for counseling. She was an attractive, seventeen-year-old girl with a rather expressionless face and a clear concise way of speaking. In the first counseling session, she explained that she had heard of the counseling services during freshman orientation week.

Miss D: They said we could probably all use some help. I don't really have any problems . . . but I suppose you want to know all about me.

C: You're not sure you really can use (Miss D. interrupts)

Miss D: I know you're not supposed to tell me anything, but . . . well . . . I'm a scholarship student here and while my marks are very good . . . well . . . I . . . I've never made any friends . . . well . . . not social friends . . . you see I don't live in a dorm.

In the first three recorded interviews, Miss D. tended to give a recital of "facts" about herself. She came from a very small town in the state and was permitted to accept the scholarship to the university if she consented to live with a married sister. She was the middle child of five sisters. Her father was dead. Her family belonged to a "fundamental" church. Miss D. spent most of the first two sessions describing school and studies. She also stated that living with her married sister made it difficult to have friends.

In the third counseling session, she appeared uncomfortable, hesitated frequently, and spoke of never having had a date. She stated that her mother praised her for not dating, but she felt that just getting good grades wasn't much fun.

Miss D: Mother never thought much about sex . . . we never
talked about it . . . though sometimes I had some fantasies
. . . I guess . . . I understand that sex *is* important to
us . . . but not to me . . . I guess I say it isn't because
I don't think men would be interested in me.

This comment ended the third session. The whole of the fourth
counseling interview follows. New ideas and changes in behavior
seemed to have occurred between these sessions. Sometimes the client
takes for granted that the counselor is aware of the events and changes.
Occasionally this makes the client's conversation a bit ambiguous,
but it is interesting to note that this ambiguity is usually clarified by
the client before the end of the session.

The Fourth Counseling Interview

Miss D. arrived on time but was breathless. Her hair was wrapped
in a scarf.

Miss D: Excuse my hair (breathless laughter). I've just come from
swimming and it's a mess.

C: (laughing also) It's embarrassing to have your hair go every
which way but the way you'd like it to go.

Miss D: Yes, it is. (Long pause, patting her hair) Oh . . . I'm so
mixed up. I had my first date last week. I don't know.
(pause) It's just everything. I mean I wasn't quite as
awkward as I thought I'd be. (pause) That wasn't the half
of it . . . (sigh) . . . If I only had used some plain common sense. (pause) All day, it was Saturday night that I went
out with him . . . and all day I was worried about it. I
knew I wouldn't know what to talk about . . . I . . . I
was concerned about it. And when he came in, well my impression of him was, well he . . . he was smaller than I
was and it made me *terribly, terribly* self-conscious. With
heels on, it made me taller and while he was nice enough,
he wasn't nasty at all, but the conversation was very strange.
And he took me to the Ice Revue which was nice . . .
and . . . so many things were interesting that I got into.
One thing—I was stupid enough to wear a real, real tight
girdle. I had never bought one for myself. This one had been
given to me . . . and I had eaten a pretty good sized

supper and considering that the girdle practically killed me
. . . spaghetti . . . So I was miserable because it cut me
right here (pointing to waistline) all through the performance. During the show he asked me if I wanted ice cream.
I thought if I had to eat another thing I'd die, but . . . so
I floundered around for a minute, and then I told him "all
right." Well, we did . . . then he took me out afterward
to a nice little place on Fourth Street with German atmosphere. You know, German-like atmosphere, lights, candles,
and all that stuff. I didn't know what he expected me to
order. I'd never had any experience like that before to tell
you the truth. I was ready to . . . I was half sick . . . so I
thought I'd get away with as little as possible; so I ordered
a sandwich and light tea (trembling with laughter), and they
gave me lemon with it, but he kept telling me about making
the tea lighter and I used all the lemon. The tea was cold by
this time, but I drank it. It was pure lemon almost. In other
words I thought I'd die. It . . . it . . . it was all I could
do to keep a straight face while I was eating. (trembling
laughter, gradually diminishes) It was awful. That was that.

C: You were mighty glad that meal was over. One discomfort
succeeded another. You just didn't know what to do. So far
the date had proved to be anything but pleasure.

Miss D: How right you are! And that was just only a small part
of it . . . then, when he took me home, we parked for
awhile. Well . . . I . . . I . . . I'm not supposed to be
naive. I mean I know what makes the world go around. At
least a little . . . but I don't have any idea about how far
to go. I think I've learned, unfortunately. I didn't know
when to tell him to stop because I didn't particularly like
any of it. I mean it wasn't particular pleasure for me, neither
did it particularly arouse me sexually . . . ah . . . I
mean . . . I think it did him, and I don't know. I think
I read about some authority saying one time that it was
easier for men to be sexually aroused and easier for them
to be satisfied than women. Whether that explains it, or
the fact that I had all this background that would sort of

sour me, or a combination of that or something altogether different . . . but I didn't particularly enjoy myself.

C: Whatever the reason, no matter how you've analyzed it, none of the lovemaking was enjoyed by you. It puzzles you.

Miss D: Yes, because I didn't know how far I ought to go because in the movies . . . ah . . . they glamorize part of it, but there's an awful lot *more* than you never see or hear told and . . . and . . . I . . . I . . . I never heard of actual, I mean, of oral contact as a substitute for sexual intercourse. I fought that because . . . I . . . ah . . . I didn't think that should be . . . but I didn't know whether I was being a prude or . . . or *what* because, as far as my own feelings were concerned, I didn't like *any* of it; so it's hard for me to know where to draw the line.

C: You find it most annoying that there is no real source of information about how you should behave. You can't even depend on your own feelings.

Miss D: That's right. Because with, with my feelings I mean, now, the effects seem to me that it's not a means in itself, but an instrument. I am more interested in a family and in a home, and the sex that would go with that would be all right, but this . . . this . . . meeting cold with a stranger like that . . .

C: Lovemaking as a casual sort of thing (Miss D. interrupts).

Miss D: Yes . . . casual sort of thing! With no satisfaction . . . So he asked, when I took him to the door, to go out with him again . . . and . . . I . . . I don't know quite why I said what I said but I . . . I wouldn't give him any definite answer because I . . . I was too, too emotional myself to think clearly at all and I . . . I . . . was afraid if I said "yes" I'd regret it and if I said "no," I'd regret it. So . . . I told him to call me on Tuesday, and I'd tell him then. So . . . (pause) I . . . When I got in the house . . . I don't quite understand why the physical hangover. I think that's one thing I didn't expect.

C: You felt shaken after the date, and that feeling you hadn't counted on.

Miss D: Hadn't counted on! My fantasies never had any, but gee whiz, I was shaken for almost an hour, I guess. I could hardly sleep. It was pretty late as it was, and I didn't get hardly any sleep at all, burning up with fever practically, and it didn't seem logical to me why it was that way.

C: You couldn't understand (Miss D. interrupts).

Miss D: Because I didn't feel very sexually aroused, while all this thing was going on. But afterwards I had all this, you know, inside. I didn't feel so good. All day Sunday I felt so . . . I couldn't keep anything in my stomach.

C: You were so upset about yourself, submitting passively to love making, that you're sick about it.

Miss D: Yes, sick. And nervous too. I . . . I didn't understand because . . . I thought that I would have had to have been aroused in order for that to happen . . . Maybe I was . . . and . . . couldn't tell the difference.

C: You're all mixed up about your feelings—whether you responded and didn't know it or whether you just submitted. You're worried because you're not sure.

Miss D: That's right. I'm not sure . . . (long pause) . . . And I really felt terrible on Monday because I felt I hadn't been discreet, and it sort of brought back that religious trouble, too. That ethics, if you want to put it that way, too. I didn't know whether I was better off not to have dated at all and just to have continued as I was . . . still (I'd hate to use the term) pure, or whether it was right for me to go ahead, even though I think it was a little licentious . . . and experiment and find out.

C: It was hard for you to decide which was more ethical: to date and experiment or not to date at all. And what you experimented with seems bad to you.

Miss D: Sort of . . . I was all day Sunday and Monday, then, trying to make up my mind: should I go out with him again or not? And I mentioned something to my sister because she'd been through it all, and I said to her that I didn't understand why I was so upset about it. And she said she thought he was a good kid and just to take it easy but to go ahead. Well . . . it took me till Tuesday evening to make up my mind whether I would go with him again or not, and I decided that I would, but *he* had left it up to *me* where we would go and I had . . . had forgotten. Well, not exactly forgotten, but just had not given it any thought—where we should go . . . and I hadn't thought of the time and all that so . . . I kinda . . . I thought all about *that*; and by that evening I still didn't know what was playing where and at what time. So I just took a rough guess about the time to tell him to come, and so I thought I'd do the best I could —I had tried Tuesday afternoon . . .

C: Dating wasn't being much fun.

Miss D: (Deep sigh) No, it wasn't. So (sigh) with all the misgivings in the world I . . . I . . . I decided to go on with it and go out with him again. I picked out a theatre and a feature that won an Academy Award . . . (pause) . . . The, I . . . Thursday, yesterday, the day he was supposed to come, and . . . again I was . . . I didn't know what to do all day Thursday because I had told him to call for me about 8 o'clock, and, when I did my phoning later, I found that the picture didn't change until 8:30, and he's a rather punctual person, and I knew that he wouldn't want to go in during the middle of the picture himself. (sigh) I didn't know whether I should call him and tell him to come later or whether I should let it ride and try to talk to him at home. (sigh) So I just decided that I would let him come around eight and hope and pray that he'd be a little late, and then I could in one way or another stall till it was time. And then I had *all* the problems at once. I didn't know what in the world to wear. I had planned on one dress and spent all Wednesday night trying to fix it, and then found I couldn't wear it. So I was flying around the last minute trying to fix something else to wear. And he came a few minutes early but, bless my sister! My sister must have known how I felt because she gave me an awfully big hand. Even my niece at two and a half (laughs) just reacted perfectly. And I don't know what I'd ever have done without them when I saw him. But when he came in, I . . . I . . . I was just a nervous wreck. Last Saturday night he was in uniform. That made me nervous. (pause) He's in the Marine Corps. He just came back from serving a year in Korea. He'd been stationed in Japan but he'd been under fire. He'll be stationed in Florida, not here. Well, when he came last night, he brought me a box of candy, and he was out of uniform, and *that* made it easier right to start off. But I didn't know what to say or what to do. But my sister came in and I introduced them. I know she's had enough experience and knows better how to handle those things. She made some decent conversation. Then he happened to see the piano and sat down and played for us for awhile. And my little niece came over. She's the type who, if a stranger picks her up, it doesn't go, but she's pretty friendly basically. And so she came over and climbed up on my lap and made me feel more secure (laughs).

C: Being surrounded with familiar people and settings made you feel less jeopardized.

Miss D: (laughs) It certainly did. (pause) So he played awhile, played some chopsticks, which was idiotic, but it did take up some time (laughing). Then we went over to the theatre, and it . . . it surprised me that I rather liked it. I got real enjoyment out of just holding his hand—more than all the other stuff. I don't quite understand why that was so, either. Saturday night I was going through all the torture and trying to think of how I should handle it . . . afterwards I thought maybe it was because I was sorta scared, and I knew I didn't respond very much on a higher level, and I figured out that was why. I thought that maybe if I responded a little bit more that would help.

C: You understand now that, not knowing how to talk to him about anything, you just allowed him the only other possible means of communicating with you.

Miss D: (emphatically) Uh, huh! (pause) Then afterwards, the movies, last night, it went too far. It went entirely too far! (pause) I was . . . was so unsure myself, of what I was doing, that I couldn't be firm in telling him when to stop . . . (pause) . . . and when I did maybe he would for a little while but then he tried it again . . . (pause) . . .

and I didn't realize how it was effecting him because it wasn't effecting *me* that way . . . (pause) . . . I wouldn't let him do that, the physical with the mouth contact again. (pause) I don't like it . . . (pause) . . . but . . . he let me almost, well, I wouldn't say *let* me because I didn't particularly want to, let me lie down completely . . . and almost take the position for intercourse . . . and I didn't know what to say or what to do because I really felt that, in a way, there wasn't much harm and yet, in a way, there was.

C: You just couldn't be sure whether it was right or not for you.

Miss D: No. I just couldn't be sure . . . A couple of times he got a little too fresh and . . . I told him to stop and . . . it seemed . . . that I couldn't think clearly myself. I didn't know what to do because I was . . . I didn't know whether to tell him to quit and take me home or what.

C: You weren't quite sure how you felt about his lovemaking.

Miss D: No. So I didn't do much of anything at all . . . for awhile . . . until he said something to me about "you're driving me insane." I thought he was just kidding, but he wasn't. I didn't get the full significance of what he was saying, what he said, and I . . . I said, I said I didn't think that it was such a good idea. He just laughed and said that some people who were crazy were pretty happy . . . (pause) . . . Well Saturday night, too, I had my coat buttoned, and he wanted to unbutton it, and I wasn't exactly sure why. Well, last night, almost before I realized it, he did it again. But still I didn't know whether I should stop it or not.

C: Even knowing what he was going to do didn't help you understand what you should do.

Miss D: No, it didn't. So that's no excuse. (pause) So, like I said, he did go a little too far. I don't think he's basically a bad person. My mother always used to say that men would go as far as you'd let them and I realize it was partly my fault too. If I had been surer of myself and told him to stop, he would have stopped. I don't understand why I didn't stop him.

C: You know, now, that you helped to create the situation for the excessive lovemaking, but you still can't understand why you didn't do more to change it.

Miss D: That's right. Because again I wasn't particularly enjoying it. But it's just that I didn't know how far to go and how far he expected me to go. I . . . I don't know what a gentleman is; so how do I know what not a gentleman is? And he wasn't being nasty . . . And my mother's warning, as I told you before, "as long as you keep your pants on, you'll be all right."

C: That wasn't much help in knowing what was right behavior for a gentleman (Miss D. interrupts).

Miss D: *No!* Not much help for me either. Because I thought either you stop it and say only kissing and that's all, and *that* was *nothing* to me. I mean, gee whiz, you're not going to sit there for a half hour or an hour or so, and that's as far as you could go.

C: You just don't believe a man would want to spend much time with you unless you went much further than just kissing.

Miss D: That's right. And I did feel that practically anything was going too far so the farther you went . . . it's just a matter of degree and . . . (outburst) well, if you go so far, you might as well go further!

C: Just doesn't seem logical to you. It exasperated you. Once you permitted him so much, there didn't seem any reason for your stopping him.

Miss D: *Yes! Yes!* (pause) And then he asked me afterwards, "Why do you let me do this to you?" That floored me. But then I thought that at least, in a way, it was pretty nice of him to say that because well, in other words, *he* was telling *me* that he thought I was letting him go too far.

C: You rather admire him for giving you a cue for your behavior, and you're sorry that you didn't pick it up (Miss D. interrupts).

Miss D: Yes, but I did.

C: You're very grateful that he helped you there.

Miss D: Yes, because I thought he didn't have to . . . ah . . . because I wouldn't have let him go much farther . . . I think . . . because I mean there is *definitely* a line. You go so far and that's it . . . but just the same I think up to that line is too far . . . (pause) . . . and so I thought . . . it at least . . . it *did* show that he had a little common sense even if I didn't—that he would say that.

C: You feel rather lucky that he knew when to stop.

Miss D: Ah. Yes. (pause) So then he took me home . . . (pause) . . . and practically the same thing happened. He asked me to go out with him again. (long pause) And I told him that I would. I don't know why I shouldn't have. (long pause) But . . . I . . . I . . . I hesitated because I thought *now* he's practically told how far he wants me to go, and maybe if I try once more, I can find out . . . if . . . if I don't want him to go so far if it's still all right.

C: If he still would want to date you.

Miss D: That's right. But still I sort of regret it because . . . (pause) . . . if all men . . . last night I was pretty sick and . . . (pause) . . . then this morning I started getting all the qualms again and thinking of all the things I was told in church and thinking that I was just using the fact that I didn't have much feeling for him . . .

C: To make it seem right to go so far.

Miss D: Yes. (pause) . . . And yet, I don't know quite what to do because of the way I was brought up in the church . . . they tell you ideally what would be fine if everybody did it. But when it comes down to practical terms . . . well . . . I don't know. The idea is that you sit all your life and wait for your Prince Charming to come, and then, when he does, it's absolutely pure so you're married, and then anything goes. But I have thought that there are some pretty nice fellows around that I could be interested in, that I might, if I knew them well enough, might consider marriage, or something like that. But I feel so inhibited, if that's the word I want to use.

C: You feel you just don't know how to be especially friendly with men.

Miss D: I felt that one way or the other . . . I felt I couldn't talk to them or feel at ease. I know that one way or another

. . . someone . . . I could learn to be at ease with him a little, and then maybe if I ever got a chance with some nicer fellows, if I weren't so awkward, I'd have a chance of making a better impression.

C: You've decided to go out again with this man because you feel that, if you can practice on someone who you wouldn't consider for marriage, you could learn the graces which you feel you lack and which keep you from making a better impression on more desirable men.

Miss D: Oh, yes! Because I did feel that if someone broke down the barriers in spite of all the bad effects it might have . . . well I could talk to him anyway . . . then, well, *that* would be an accomplishment.

C: If you once could get started chatting, even after the sex play, you could talk to him as a person. It was worth the risk to you.

Miss D: That's it! (emphatically) I think that, perhaps, part of my old fear of talking with him was the fear of sex—because it was sort of unknown to me. And I didn't know how to solve anything like that. And I felt uncomfortable, and I was afraid to trust myself, too, because . . . I wasn't particularly *labelled* that, but *I felt queer* because I had never dated, and it seems now, after these dates, to make me even with the other girls, to put me more on their level.

C: Despite all the doubts and fears, the two dates have made you feel more acceptable, more normal with girls you know.

Miss D: Yes. (pause) And then again that has had its religious repercussions, too, because that is . . . ah . . . ah a kind of worldly, getting on in the world. You're supposed to be *separated,* the *Chosen.* But I don't know whether it's better to be miserable and one of the chosen or to be otherwise and not . . . because I . . . I still can't get over this feeling that religions—I don't know whether it is fanaticism or not—but I'm afraid. Their religion is so impossible that I don't see *how* it can be right. They . . . they say it's the only right way, but even if you get them to define their terms it doesn't work.

C: Being one of the chosen sounds rather like an impossible way of living for you.

Miss D: Yes. You have to be perfect! But nobody can be perfect. So then they tell you that you can strive to be perfect. So does that mean that you basically decide that good is the right way and that, in a reasonable sense, you don't do excesses in any way?

C: You're wondering whether it is possible to live by the words of the elder's even though you doubt it.

Miss D: That's my interpretation of it. At least that's the way I like to interpret it . . . (pause) . . . or whether, like their interpretations, you just see how many things you could cut down and how many things you could say are worldly so that the more things you give up, the more that signifies that you're holy? And so they end up with a few of their people being holy and the rest of us . . .

C: You don't believe that you could be that holy, that very few people could be.

Miss D: I don't believe it. And I think it's bad for both kinds. It makes drunks and the opposite excess out of them because somebody, not too well-balanced, to try so long in his religion and . . . well, he gets frustrated because he doesn't get anywhere, and then he flies completely off. That's the way I relate it to the whole question of how I'm ever going to adjust to sex.

C: You don't want to be the extreme at either end.

Miss D: No, I don't. Because I remember in our church, well . . . it's not so much what I remember as what I've been told by my sisters . . . that young people in our church are not well-adjusted. My sister was the wholly proper, and everything else you could name, outcast. The conventional sinner as far as all the pious people in the church were concerned. Actually, she was better balanced than they, and she wouldn't bow down to them. The other kids would go up to the altar and get saved, and then they would go out for a week feeling they were being very holy. And then they had the approval of the whole church. But then they would go off and do as they pleased and, if they were found out, they would just go up to the altar again and get saved all over again. Everything would be all right again. My sister used a lot more common sense. She decided that she was going to be a little more normal and have a little fun living. So she went to this camp in Indiana. It was a horror. I was there myself when I was small. It's a place where you're supposed to love to go to church from the minute you get out of bed in the morning to the minute you go to sleep at night. And everything is on a strict schedule. No recreation for the kids at all, hardly. You can work your way through if you want to. There's dishwashing. You get real enlightenment between dishwashing and church services. And, once in awhile, you can go to town, to the crossroads where there is a candy store and a gas station. So when my sister was around, I suppose, say sixteen, she was very pretty. Her father is Irish; and, you know, she had the lightest coloring and everything and long hair. She was *very, very* popular with the kids in their neighborhood. She didn't get out much. Mother kept her home working all the time, most of the time with us kids. We were all small at once. Well, she went to this camp, and she would sneak off and go boating, which was *forbidden,* like the rest of the kids would. But this one time, a whole gang of them went together, and then they were caught while they were in the boat together. They were brought back, and I don't know what all happened before those pious elders of the church. They were called everything from heaven to hell and back again. I suppose not really in a profane way. At least pious people wouldn't have considered it profane. And they told them about how they were so sinful and worldly and all this business. So more so than the other girls; in fact, most of them would just break down in tears sobbing all over the place that they were sinners, that they were sorry. But my sister said, "I'm not a sinner. I did it and I'm glad and that's all there is to it." She said, "And if I'm sorry, that's my business. I'm not confessing to you. And I don't believe in that. I wanted to have fun and I had fun. I didn't do anything wrong, and I'm not going to say I did anything wrong." So that's the type of background she had. She's made a rather good adjustment to life, and she's taken the whole thing pretty much in perspective. She won't advise me much, but she seems always able to say the right word at the right time. That . . . I . . . I . . . There couldn't have been, I don't think, any better circumstances for all these happenings because she was so sympathetic, and she did have quite a bit of experience, and she had a background similar to what I had. There's a lot of differences too, but they're all just incidental. Most of the important things are the same. She didn't get out much until she started to date, even younger than I did, but not so terribly much. I think she had a nicer, a little more personality than I had. It was more open. But she understands; and when I told her how upset I was, she said, "Yes, I know. But you've got to find out sometime." So (sigh), I've, I've just come out of it all with a . . . I can sort of look objectively at the way I was taught.

C: These experiences have made it possible for you to examine old learnings.

Miss D: Yes. Yes, and see well . . . those geezers were pretty strict, but, well, I bet they must have sowed some wild oats too. And my mother too in a much milder form, she can be sorta strict and say how proud she is that none of her girls run around but *that's* no compliment to me. (pause) And yet she married at seventeen and had a child before she was married more than a few months and had two of them and a divorce by the time she was nineteen; and *then* she did plenty of running around; and then she finally married my dad; and she was never quite in love with him. I mean not till she lived with him quite a long time. When she was first married to him, she wasn't at all faithful to him. So now she regrets *that*. So when we were really too small to understand, she built up all this fear in us. That's one thing that . . . that sort of surprised me that there's nothing to be afraid of particularly. I mean if you don't go too far, *which I did!* It upset me because I don't think I should have, but I'll never be half as afraid again about just talking or something like that.

C: You've gained something out of all the pain of the experience. You're not likely ever to be afraid of men as you were. You're not sorry that it happened.

Miss D: Yes. That's really the way I feel about it. (pause) I'm awfully glad that I could come and talk with you about it because I . . . I . . . everything was whirling around in my head. I didn't know which way to turn. (pause) It was just miraculous, too, to me, the help my sister gave me. I don't really believe I appreciated her until all this came up.

C: It was wonderful to have someone around who understood (Miss D. interrupts).

Miss D: Yes, because I feel that there's too big an age gap between my mother and myself. She just had time to regret too much. I'm not quite sure what all was involved, but my mother didn't come out of it quite as enlightened as my sister has and will. I think my sister always will be a much better balanced person than my mother because . . . (pause) . . . Ah . . . I don't know whether my mother wasn't quite as strong a character as my sister, or what. Or whether it was partly because she wasn't exposed to education either. My sister is a very enlightened person because of all the education she got. I mean so much that . . .

C: You feel that an education can make you more understanding.

Miss D: No, it's not so much that, but she's got a good idea of the world. She's tried everything, and she knows more of the true values in life than, I think, my mother does.

C: You'd much rather be like her than your mother.

Miss D: Of course. Even my mother leaned on her an awful lot. She matured very quickly. And she just does know how to say the right thing at the right time, or how not to say the wrong things, or not to say anything on occasion.

C: You admire your sister's poise, her knowing (Miss D. interrupts).

Miss D: I do. And I think part of the reason was that, in *spite* of all that horror name-calling that she got from the church, that her theory was, "I'll try it. And I'll go into it objectively, knowing what I've seen of the outcomes from other people, and if I think it's worth hanging on to, I'll do it in spite of what they think, and if I don't think it has any value, I won't do it."

C: What you admire about your sister is that she does what she believes to be best for her, her considered judgment (Miss D. interrupts).

Miss D: Yes, uh huh.

C: (Continues) and isn't coerced into doing what she doesn't want to do or feels isn't right for her.

Miss D: Oh, yes! Because I feel that coercion in my life so much. Sometimes I just stop and think if I could *only* do what *I* think is best. If *I* only didn't have all this weight of what people told me, "*This* way or you'll go to Hell." Because *they don't know* what they're talking about.

C: You so much want to be a free agent, and yet you still feel caught by what others tell you to do.

Miss D: Oh, yes! (pause) And, yet from time to time, the cradle up practically, these pious people of the church, most of them, like I said, did sow their wild oats—there have been enough of them through the ages that they know the vice of the world. They know best how to counteract it, a sort of reverse psychology before it ever hits you. So before I ever knew anything about what it would be like to park or anything like that, I had all these attitudes built up first that they had given to me about sin, about vice on the altar of modernism and worldliness. Before I had ever danced, I had heard over and over repetition of pretty awful things, about how dance halls were hell halls. Well, a lot of things they preach against I agree are *wrong*. But if only they'd go about it a little differently.

C: Some of the things the elders thought were bad you believed were bad too, but you feel the way they did it only made you more, more (Miss D. interrupts).

Miss D: Yes, more curious.

C: And so you just had to find out for yourself.

Miss D: Yes . . . for myself.

C: Just to see, to check. (pause) Our time is up for today. Some time next week?

Miss D: Yes, please. (pause, long sigh) So much happens between these times. (pause) Goodbye.

C: Goodbye.

Miss Dha continued for eight more sessions. She joined a number of university clubs, one of them a religious group. Within six months she was engaged to a young church worker whom she has since married. Two years after the counseling sessions were ended, she was seen again. Her most illuminating comment concerning counseling was:

Miss D: I was pretty lucky I didn't get into any real mess. The most wonderful part was finding out that I was pretty much like everybody else. Of course, John thinks I'm very different (but very nice). I know I'm going to be a lot more natural with my daughter and have her know a lot about boys all the time so she can find out they're just people, even though sometimes they can be very special people.

Discussion

The primary function of the non-directive counselor is to provide an emotional climate within which the client can grow in self-understanding. To do this, the counselor must honestly accept the client's statements, attitudes, and actions. Even more important, the counselor must convey to the client this acceptance. A client-centered counselor is convinced that the client has the capacity for self-understanding and problem solving; consequently the counselor will refrain from giving advice or actively intervening in the client's life. This is not always easy. There were times in my counseling of Miss Dha when I felt that I could have been of help in a more active way. Yet, being convinced that Miss Dha could gain the greatest benefits from solving her own problems, I refrained from giving advice. In reading over my comments, it will be noted that they fall primarily into two categories: the restatement of the content of Miss Dha's expressions and the clarification of Miss Dha's feelings.

Counselors are frequently at a loss to know how they should react to problems in the sexual or religious areas. It seems to me that the client-centered technique (or what the author of this book calls the client-centered-non-directive technique) is of particular benefit in these areas. I am not convinced that any counselor has the answers to questions in these areas. If this is true, then most certainly the counselor should not give advice. To carry this reasoning a step further, it seems doubtful to me that the counselor can ever know his client well enough to know what should be done with his life. That is to say, no matter how much information we can accumulate about an individual, I do not believe that we can ever know another individual sufficiently well to make his decisions for him. I realize that few counselors would admit that they attempt to make decisions for others; however, there are many subtle ways in which the counselor can influence the decision making process. For example, giving approval or withholding approval of a counselee's plans or actions, in effect amounts to aiding the counselee in making a decision. It will be noted, that at no time did I convey directly or indirectly to Miss Dha that I approved or disapproved of her actions. It might be asked what I would have done if Miss Dha had told me that she was actually going to have intercourse with her boy friend as part of her social growth. My answer would be the same. I personally would not have thought it wise, which is another way of saying that I would not have done the same thing myself. However, Miss Dha's need was not to understand me but to understand herself. I would have, in other words, continued to react to Miss Dha's statements in the same manner as I had done previously. It is very important to understand that this attitude of mine is predicated upon a deep conviction of not only the right but the ability of the individual to help himself. This process may involve making mistakes, but the mistakes themselves may be a very important part of the growth process.

There is one last point which must be considered. Do all individuals, that is at all age, intellectual, and emotional levels, have the same ability to solve their problems? I must admit that I am not sure of the answer to this question. Certainly we need research in this area. I am convinced, however, that counselors should assume that this ability is possessed to a far greater degree than many are willing to admit.

22...

I Love You Counselor

Lucy was a seventeen-year-old, eleventh-grade girl whose intelligence and standardized achievement test scores indicate that she possesses less than average ability. She was referred to the guidance office because of poor work in her classes. When she came into my office, she seemed to be on the verge of tears. As her poor achievement did not really seem to warrant her extreme emotional upset, I asked her if there was some problem that was bothering her. She literally poured out her heart to me saying that her step-father hated her, had called her a tramp, and continually beat her and shouted at her. The situation had become so intolerable that she was afraid to go home. Further, Lucy's mother was unaware of her step-father's cruelty as the incidents had occurred when her mother was absent. She was afraid to tell her mother because it would only lead to a fight between her parents. Lucy stated that she was planning to quit school, get a job, and leave home as soon as possible. I told Lucy that I could understand why she was upset and asked her to come back on the following day when we would have some additional time to talk. Before she left, she said that it had been wonderful to be able to speak with me because I seemed interested in her problems and did not laugh at her.

The next day Lucy brought up another problem. It seemed that her boy friend (eighteen-years-old) had been killed in a plane crash while he was in the service. She was still mourning his loss, and now his brother had asked her to go out with him. Lucy wanted to know what to do. We discussed the question of her feelings concerning the dead youth and his brother. I was as noncommittal as possible and attempted to get her to verbalize her own feelings as fully as possible. Actually Lucy's comments called for little responsiveness on my part, and she seemed more than satisfied to just have me listen.

An Unforeseen Problem

After several weeks Lucy came in again. She handed me a letter requesting that I read it. She said that she wasn't able to tell me verbally what she had said in the letter but that she would come in the next day and talk with me.

Lucy's letter went as follows:

Dear Mr. ——,

It's too bad you're my counselor because I really like you. I told my Aunt how I felt, and she said that it was only a teen-age crush and that I would get over it. But I don't feel that way at all. Because every time I see you (and that's mostly every period of the day) Mr. ——, when you talk to me I don't know what to do, I get so tongue tied I don't know what to do or say. My heart aches for some one like you to hold me in his arms. You once said that you would rather have respect than likeness, well I have both for you. Mr. ——, I don't even know your first name, but I'm sure it's a nice one, besides any name would fit you. I hope someday my dreams will all come true. And if they don't, I pray and wish that the one I love will be as wonderful as you.

Love always now and forever,
Lucy

Needless to say I had some doubts as to how to handle my next session with Lucy. I'm sure that it was a somewhat painful and embarrassing meeting for both of us. When Lucy came in, I told her that I was happy that she had felt free to express her feelings and that I did value her friendship. I asked her if perhaps her feeings might not have been caused by my being the first one she had come to after the death of her boy friend. She replied that she had thought of this but that she did not believe that this was the case. I tried to be as honest as I could and told her that, while I hoped that we could continue to be friends, our relationship would have to remain that of counselor and student. She accepted this without further comment.

At the end of this conference, I surmised that perhaps I had seen the last of Lucy in my office; however, several days later she came in. She said that she had a "real problem." Her girl friend had gone to the doctor and had received a verdict of cancer of the breast. The girl's only chance of a cure was to have her breast removed. She did not want to tell her mother because they were in poor financial straits; also, she did not want to become a "shapeless woman." Lucy wanted to know what she should do—keep her friend's problem a secret or tell the girl's mother. I discussed the situation with Lucy and left the decision up to her.

Discussion

Lucy presented a problem which may arise in many counseling careers. There will be times, I am sure, when the counselee will honestly fall in love with her, or his, counselor. Lucy was a little more difficult problem for me because, being single, I could not hide behind the fact that I was married. Also, the discrepancy in our ages amounted to less than seven years. I do not believe that Lucy's affection for me was very deep; however, it could have developed into quite a problem. I believe that the situation was caused by a set of circumstances: lack of home understanding, the death of a boy friend, school pressures, and the discovery of an individual with whom she could talk freely. I think that I was fortunate that Lucy brought her feelings out into the open where they could be examined. I did not have the slightest idea that she thought she was in love with me. Perhaps, if I had been more acute in my observations, I might not have been taken unawares. Regardless of this, I wonder if I handled the situation correctly. Frankly, I do not know of how else I could have met the problem. It seems to me that in a situation such as this, honesty is most definitely the best policy. As Lucy was able to come back again for another session, the problem apparently did not interfere with the counseling relationship.

There is, of course, another issue in this case. What would I have done if Lucy's girl friend had been my counselee? I am inclined to believe that ethically, a counselor should check the veracity of such a story with the girl's physician and then urge the counselee to inform her parents. If this fails, I believe the counselor should then take direct action with the home. Actually, in this particular case, I believe that Lucy was using the problem as an excuse to come in and see me. She was trying to show me that she still had confidence in me even though I had rebuffed her show of affection. I believe that the physician involved would most definitely inform the girl's parents of the fact that she had cancer. Perhaps, I am reading too much between the lines of Lucy's comments, but I did have the distinct impression that she was not too seriously concerned with the situation.

I have one last comment to make. The affectional relationship which developed could have been avoided if we had had a woman counselor as part of our staff. Perhaps, a good solution would be to employ a woman and a man as half time counselors rather than to just have one full time counselor who may have to face difficulties which arise because of his, or her, sex.

23...

You're Supposed To Help Us

Leslie was sixteen years old and in the tenth grade. As she was failing typing, health, and English, she had been requested to come in for an interview to see what might be done to help her attain better grades.

I have two roles in our high school: that of a guidance counselor and that of an English instructor. Leslie was a member of my slowest group in English. Her I.Q. on two intelligence tests was low normal. Her attempts to master the subject matter in my class were disorganized and sporadic. She was constantly trying to dominate the classroom discussion and seemed to talk mostly to hear herself talk. She rarely thought before she spoke and often asked questions which made little sense—an indication that she had not been paying attention. Leslie was, in short, an extremely irritating student.

This was my first year as a guidance counselor, and I had never had any formal training in counseling principles and procedures. Therefore, I was extremely apprehensive about every move that I made. I was concerned about inviting Leslie to come in for an interview because, frankly, I disliked her as a student. I wondered if I would be able to modify my feelings toward her in the counseling situation.

When she entered my office, I asked her to sit down and explained that I was seeing all of the sophomores who were experiencing difficulty with their studies. I asked her why she thought that she had failed three subjects. She replied that she felt her failures were due to home conditions. I then asked her if she could explain this in more detail. She evaded the issue by again replying that it was impossible to study at home. Since the tone of her voice was decidedly hostile,

I felt that nothing could be gained by asking further questions pertaining to her home life. I changed the subject and suggested some standard study procedures that she might follow in preparing her homework. We discussed a few of these points; and then I asked her if she thought there was anything that she might improve in her classroom behavior. She replied that she realized that she should think before she spoke, but she just couldn't seem to stop herself. I told her that this was, indeed, a problem that she shared with many, many people. We talked over this problem, and I concluded the interview by saying that if she wished to speak with me further about her work, or anything else, I would be more than happy to listen, and I would try to help in any way that I could.

The following day Leslie was extremely quiet in class, and I was concerned for I was afraid that perhaps our previous discussion had completely blocked her self-expression. However, she came to me after lunch and asked for an excuse from her next class so that she might talk with me. As she seemed upset, I readily agreed to see her.

The Problem

When she came into my office, she was extremely tense, and so I directed the conversation toward her interests. She revealed that she was very active in church work. I asked her if she had ever spoken to her minister about the things that bothered her. Leslie replied, "No, he is too old and I don't think he would understand what I could tell him." Then she started to cry. After about three minutes, I asked her if she would like to tell me what was making her so unhappy. She began to talk in a halting manner. "My father is really taking advantage of me, and I'm scared about what's going to happen." As I wasn't certain that I had correctly interpreted what she was telling me, I asked her if she could explain what she meant in a little more detail. In a fast and almost toneless voice, she replied that her father would come into her room almost every evening, lock the door, and force her to have intercourse with him. I asked her where her mother and brother were during this time. She told me that her mother worked in a factory on the night shift and that her brother was usually out running around. She also indicated that she and her mother were not close and that it would be impossible for her to talk with her mother about her father's actions.

As I was completely bewildered about what course of action to take, I explained to her that I would like a little time to think of a way to help her. I also asked her to return to my office at the close of the day. She agreed to return and seemed somewhat more relieved as she left to return to her classes.

Our principal had been handling school problems for many years, and so I went to him for advice. I explained the situation to him and asked him what he thought should be done. Also, I indicated that, although I felt Leslie was telling the truth, there was the possibility that she might be lying. He said that he had had a few cases like this before and had always referred them to the local police. He then continued to say that since we had little way of knowing the truth of Leslie's accusations, it would be best to accept them at face value.

After talking with our principal, I called the Chief of Police and requested an appointment. He was able to see me at once, and so I left for his office immediately. When he learned of the nature of Leslie's problem, he said that the only protection which could be offered would involve quite a drastic move. Court action would have to be taken so that she could be removed from her home. If this was to be done, she would have to testify against her father. I told him that I could see that this would be a most difficult decision for a young girl to make and added that I felt that Leslie might be hesitant about assuming such a responsibility. I then asked him about the possibility of utilizing the aid of a caseworker; however, he felt that this would be useless since the caseworker would eventually run up against the same wall. He stated that this was a decision that Leslie would have to make by herself and that he would be happy to talk with her later in the afternoon.

When Leslie returned to my office, I explained to her that I had spoken to the Chief of Police and also informed her of the possible course of action that was open to her. I asked her if she would like to speak with him. She seemed most anxious to do so.

The Chief of Police spoke with Leslie alone for about half an hour and then saw me, also separately. At this time he told me he was convinced that she was telling the truth and also stated that he had checked on her father and had learned that he was notorious for his promiscuous behavior. He added that he felt Leslie would not take court action and that the only thing to do was to wait until "something tragic" happened.

I drove Leslie home and asked her to think over what the Chief had said. I also asked her to come to see me if she wished to discuss it further and to be certain to let me know when she decided what she wanted to do.

She did not come back to my office until a week later. When she entered, she seemed well in control of her emotions and stated immediately that she had decided to "let things go." She did not want to take action against her father as it would break up her parents' marriage, and marriage she felt was a "holy institution." I asked her what she thought she could do about her home situation. Leslie replied, "I have no idea, Miss ——; nothing can help me, and I just don't care anymore. You're supposed to be here to help us, and you haven't done one thing for me." I told her that while I could give her some advice, she was the only one who could help herself. Then I suggested that she should certainly lock her door at night and refuse to open it to her father. I also said that she should make every effort to develop a closer relationship with her mother and should try to persuade her to change to the day shift. I asked her if she would like me to speak with her mother about her inability to study at home. Leslie replied that her mother disliked any interference from the school. She went on to indicate that her mother had quite negative feelings about Leslie even going to school for she felt that the girl should be working at a full time job. I pursued the subject no further.

As I closed the session, I told Leslie that I hoped she would feel free to stop in and see me whenever she wanted to. Then I asked her to return in two weeks and let me know how she was progressing with the suggestions that I had given her.

At the end of the two weeks, Leslie returned. She told me that as far as her relationship with her mother went, she had not had much success and that she felt she never would. However, she was locking her door each night; and because of the complaints of the neighbors, her father, although furious with her, had stopped banging on it and shouting at her. Three months passed before I again saw Leslie in my office.

Leslie's marks continued to be poor, and her classroom behavior continued to be most unacceptable. I now realized that this was an insecure girl's bid for attention. However, although I was sympathetic, I was beginning to reach the end of my patience for she was continually disrupting the class. She seemed to feel that the class time was hers alone, and she was quite intolerant of the ideas of other class members.

Then one day she came into my office and told me that her mother had been placed on the day shift. This was entirely a factory decision and had not come from any change of attitude in the home. Leslie also said that she was now employed part time and that she was dating a boy whom she liked quite a bit. Her father even approved as the boy had "a lot of money and a big car." Then she said, "I know you don't like me very much Miss ——, and I wish I could do better in English." I asked her why she thought I disliked her, and she replied, "You think I'm mean because I try to show the kids in class how silly the things they say are. They're all dumb kids anyway, and they're never going to get anywhere but this hick town." I tried to explain to her that I did not personally dislike any of my students. However, I did feel that the other students were entitled to their opinions, just as she was. Then I tried to show her that she could gain nothing by ridiculing the ideas of others. I suggested that if she would try to organize her thoughts a little more, she might be able to present her ideas in a more favorable light. I added that I thought that she really wanted her classmates to like her and told her that she could not gain their friendship without first offering her own. She replied that, since she was a good Christian, she liked everyone but that no one except her boyfriend liked her. We continued to talk further about this problem with no real gains being made.

In Leslie's junior year in high school, her academic work continues to be about the same. However, she has joined some clubs and seems to be better liked by her peers.

Discussion

After having Leslie as one of my first counseling cases, I wonder about the wisdom of using an untrained person as a guidance counselor. While my previous experience as a teacher was extremely valuable, I most definitely was not trained to handle a case such as Leslie's. If I had better understood Leslie, I am certain that my negative feeling towards this girl would not have existed, or, at least would have been minimized. I was insecure in my counseling role and now realize that Leslie must have sensed this. Unfortunately, there was no one to whom I could refer Leslie so I did the best I could. Of course, part of my problem was my dual role as counselor-teacher. There are many times when I feel that this role is a definite asset; i.e., I am able to know the child before she comes to my office. In Leslie's case the dual role was a definite handicap. I believe I could have worked more effectively with her if I had not had her as a student. I had no genuine affection for Leslie, and she was sensitive enough to realize this. Although I feel I did help her, at least to some extent, I am equally certain that I could have been of greater assistance if I had been able to demonstrate a more affectionate attitude toward her. Leslie needed someone with whom a genuine relationship could have been established.

Another question which comes to my mind concerns the legal aspects of this case. There should have been some manner in which Leslie could be protected without forcing her to initiate action. Perhaps, I should have asked the Chief of Police to call the father in and talk with him. This might have been a sufficient deterrent to his behavior. On the other hand, there is the possibility that he would then have taken out his spite on Leslie. I am convinced that the school should not have become any more involved than it was.

There is one other area of concern here. I believe that much of Leslie's reluctance to take legal action was because of her religious belief in the sanctity of marriage. I am sure that her religious beliefs have also caused some deep guilt feelings and, very likely, irreparable damage in the area of future marital sexual satisfaction. I did not attempt to counsel in this area for two reasons. First of all, my own beliefs in this area are quite different than Leslie's; and secondly, I am not certain that a school counselor should become involved with matters of religion. Quite frequently, religious questions arise in counseling sessions, and I wonder how they should be handled.

24...
What Shall I Do?

Last spring I received the following letter:

Dear Miss——,

I am a former counselee of yours, I graduated from high school two years ago. I went to New York to work as a secretary but had to quit last month because I am expecting a baby. The father of the baby is a boy I have been dating since high school. He is a neighbor of ours at home. We had been practically engaged. Now that I am pregnant, he refuses to marry me or to see me.

I'm now living at home. Both my mother and step-father work, and I have a younger brother in school. My step-father is angry about the whole situation. I have no money to prepare for the baby, and I don't want to be a burden or cause a fuss at home.

Please write to me and tell me what I should do.

Sincerely,

Ellen

After reading the letter several times, I called Ellen on the phone. We made an appointment for her to come to my office to discuss the situation. Talking with Ellen at our first session, I found out that Jerry, her boy friend, had promised to marry Ellen when they had first discovered that she was pregnant. They then went to the doctor's for various tests; but before entering the doctor's office, Jerry told Ellen that he was not ready for marriage. After this he turned and left. The next time that Ellen saw Jerry was at Sunday School. He ignored her completely.

Ellen turned to her family, but they felt that they had enough financial responsibility. As Ellen could not help support herself or contribute to the maintenance of the home, her step-father was not at all pleased with the whole situation. "What should I do?" she asked.

We talked over the several alternatives to the situation. Ellen could keep house for the family, have her child, and stay at home. Ellen was not in favor of this as she thought that she would be a burden and that her step-father would dislike her and her child. Ellen could go to a home for "unwed mothers." Actually this was what Ellen had in mind when she came to me, and she wanted addresses of places to which she could go. However, as I talked with Ellen, I became convinced that she did not really want to go away from those she loved and to face her problem alone. There were several other alternatives; she could have the child and give it up for adoption. She could go to an aunt's house, have the baby there, and not disgrace the family.

The final solution that Ellen decided upon was to stay at home, borrow any necessary money, and then repay it as soon as possible. Ellen did not think her mother would let her pay back the borrowed money so she decided that she would, when able, buy appliances which were needed in the home and present them to her mother in the form of gifts. She also realized that she and the baby would have to make a special effort to win over her step-father.

Outcome of the Case

Ellen remained in the community, continued to go to church, and her family tried to help in every way that they could. Early in the fall I received a birth announcement—a little girl. Several weeks after this Ellen called to say that Kathy had "taken over" the home. Her step-father thought there was no other baby in the world like Kathy. Jerry had escaped from the situation by entering the service. At the present time, Ellen is earning money at home by doing typing and ironing for people. She also takes care of the house and gets the meals. Recently she bought her mother a new automatic washer, a welcome addition to the household.

What the future holds for Ellen I do not know. I do feel that she has faced her problem and is happier and wiser for having done so.

Discussion

Although Ellen's case has a favorable outcome, it raises many questions concerning the problems a counselor may meet in handling the cases of unwed mothers. Most certainly the counselor will need to examine his attitudes concerning illegitimacy. In many instances, the boy involved is forced to marry the girl. Probably sufficient pressure could have been put on Jerry to force him to marry Ellen. I do not believe that this type of problem should be necessarily "solved" in such a manner. If the couple involved are not ready for marriage, then it seems to me that the problems created are not solved by a shotgun-procedure. I personally believe that Ellen is far better off for not having married Jerry. In other words, it seems to me that the ultimate welfare of all concerned, including the baby, was better served by not forcing a marriage that was repugnant to at least one of the marital partners.

Every school year, counselors will find some of their girls coming to them with Ellen's problem. How should the problem be handled? I realize that the answer to this will depend upon the individual case; however, I have seen many lives ruined as a result of such situations. Public attitudes, particularly in the small community, can make life unbearable for an unwed mother and an illegitimate child.

There may come a time when the counselor is questioned concerning the possibility of an abortion. What should the answer be? I realize that there is both an ethical and legal problem here, but I can not close my eyes to the fact that abortions are done and sometimes under indirect medical sanction. Be that as it may, how should a counselor answer a query in this area? What is the responsibility of a school counselor in notifying parents and the administration of the school of the girl's problem?

I believe that one contribution which a counselor can make is in the area of attitudes. If a counselor, because of personal convictions and beliefs, is unable to accept girls such as Ellen in a calm, understanding and noncondemning manner, then this counselor is not suited for this type of counseling. As the counselor is frequently the initial contact for a very frightened girl, it is imperative that this initial contact be a good one.

25...

Please Help Me

Lee was a fourteen-year-old high school girl. She had been born to parents who had been united in a "shotgun-marriage." Lee's parents separated when she was three years old. Since that time, she and her mother lived with her maternal grandparents. Lee indicated that her grandparents had served as parents and that she and her mother had never been particularly close.

Apparently the parental separation had not affected Lee's intellectual and social growth. Scholastic records indicated that Lee had exceptional ability and had demonstrated high achievement in her school work. Sociometric devices showed that Lee was a very popular girl with her classmates.

As indicated, Lee had been raised within her grandparents' home. In addition to her mother, two uncles also resided there. The relationship between Lee and her uncles had been most warm. They gave Lee a considerable amount of attention and affection. Lee also had a ten-year-old brother who had been born out of wedlock. She got along well with her brother, and there was no more than the usual amount of sibling rivalry.

Lee had been referred to me by her homeroom teacher who had begun to notice a decided change in her behavior, dress, and attitude. In her first contact with me, Lee was reticent to talk and maintained that nothing was wrong with her. I did not challenge this statement but released her to return to her classroom with the comment that if anything arose in her life for which she felt the need of a confidant, to please return to see me at any time.

Counseling

Lee returned to my office, voluntarily, a week later. Her head was bent low, and she seemed disturbed and nervous. With a little encouragement, she proceeded to blurt out her problem. She was two months pregnant. She had not told her mother for fear of the wrath which would descend upon her. She told me that she felt that she had let everyone down. All of her friends and relatives held her in such high esteem. Throughout her school years she had been an outstanding pupil, winning a number of competitive awards; her family expected great things from her; now she had let them down. Further, Lee revealed, her mother had had to leave high school due to a pregnancy and had looked forward to the day when her daughter would rectify her misdeed and receive a high school diploma. Now, after only a year in high school, she had failed everyone. I offered her my handkerchief and let her cry quietly for a few moments. Then, in as calm a voice as I could muster, I told her that while this was a serious thing it was not the end of the world, that many girls had had the same problem, and, that while painful, the problem could be resolved. I then went on to tell her that I thought it was unwise to withhold the facts from her mother. I inquired as to whether the boy involved would assume any responsibility. I found that he was seventeen years old, had no way of helping financially, and had no intention of assuming any responsibility. He had stopped seeing Lee as soon as he had learned of her condition. I concluded the session by telling Lee to tell her mother of her pregnancy over the weekend and to return to my office on Monday.

Lee came into my office, on Monday, in a most belligerent mood. She told me of a very stormy weekend. Her mother wanted her to get an abortion. Lee had agreed and then refused. Her change of mind had come after she had talked with her grandmother. Her grandmother had informed her of how dangerous an abortion could be and had also emphasized the immoral nature of such an act. When Lee informed her mother that she would not have an abortion, maternal wrath descended upon her. I also found out that the young Lothario in the case had left town to avoid being available should legal action be taken.

As Lee talked, her belligerent attitude subsided. Knowing that she was still very confused and in need of comfort and help, I immediately arranged via the telephone, to talk with her mother in my office that afternoon. It seemed to me that action should be taken immediately, that there was no reason to delay. As Lee left my office her parting remark was, "Please help me out of this mess; it won't happen again, please!"

Lee's mother came into my office as requested. She seemed hurt and stunned over what had happened and could not understand how Lee could have done such a thing. She began to cry. After a few moments, I told her that it seemed to me that she should consider the manner in which she had raised her daughter. She said that Lee had always been permitted to do the things that made her happy. At an early age, Lee had gone to dances and parties, and she had never objected to Lee's boyfriends. She had always given her what she wanted, and now Lee had betrayed her. At this point I intervened. I pointed out to her that, as parents, we are frequently blind to the needs of our children. In our very attempts to make our children happy, we sometimes overlook the fact that they are also human, that they are subject to the same temptations and stumbling blocks with which we were confronted in our maturational years. I told her that her own experiences should have made her particularly sensitive to Lee's problem. "Did you," I asked, "talk with Lee about problems in the sexual area?" She had not. I then went on to tell her that Lee's action could not be undone, that she should consider whether or not she might have contributed to the problem, and that she should now consider how the problem could be handled so that Lee's life would not be unnecessarily ruined. She seemed to accept what I was saying. I then said that there were several ways in which the problem could be treated. I told her that I thought an abortion was a very unwise solution because it was not only dangerous but illegal as well. Consequently, there were two possible solutions: Lee could discontinue her schooling for the present, and have the baby and place it for adoption, and then return to school in the following year; or, Lee could have the baby and not return to school. This would mean that she would assume the full-time responsibilities of motherhood. I added that, because of Lee's age, the first solution seemed to me to be the best one. Mrs.——— said that she needed time to think.

I called Lee into my office, with her mother still present, and repeated my suggestions. Both Lee and her mother seemed relieved to have had some suggestions for positive action. Her mother asked for an appointment for the following week. At that time she came in and told me that they had decided that Lee would have the baby at home, place the child for adoption when it was born; at this time Lee would then return to school.

Discussion

I make no apologies for the manner in which I handled Lee's case. There are times, in my opinion, when a counselor must be most directive. I believe that pregnancy counseling with unwed minors is an excellent example of such a case. I think that a counselor can be understanding, sympathetic, and supportive; and, at the same time, be firm and directive in his actions. Further, I believe that, while Lee will have all of our social mores to fight, in time she will make an emotional adjustment and that this incident will not ruin her life.

There are several other questions which can be asked with respect to this case. If Lee had decided to have an abortion, what would have been my responsibility as a counselor with respect to having this information? Legally I know what *should be* done. Ethically, considering the total welfare of the counselee, I think there is room for a difference of opinion as to what *should be* done. This is an issue which a counselor should carefully consider in the light of its legal and moral implications.

There are counselors who might feel that cases, such as Lee's should be placed in the hands of legal or welfare authorities. I do not believe that this should be done. There will, of course, be exceptions to this statement; but generally the fewer people involved, the easier it is for the girl to go through the experience without it leaving residual emotional scars.

26...
It Was A
Happy Marriage

Nancy was an attractive, well-groomed girl in her early thirties. She came to my office because she had heard from some friends that I did counseling, "but not of the head-shrinking variety." I smiled at her comment and asked her to be seated. "Why do you feel you need counseling?" I asked. In brief, her story was as follows.

Some fourteen years prior to this time Nancy had fallen in love with a young professional man. According to Nancy, it was a happy marriage. They had similar interests. They went to plays, liked the same friends, and seldom argued. "I never had the slightest doubt that John loved me. I still love him," she said. "One day, out of the clear blue sky, he asked me for a divorce. I was stunned and pleaded with him to change his mind but he wouldn't." She paused momentarily to gain control over her voice and then went on to say that John had remarried almost immediately, moved from the community, and was now living in another city with his wife and small son. "I know the failure of our marriage was all my own fault. That's what makes it so hard to live with. I just can't believe that I've really lost him. I still want him back."

"Why do you feel that your marriage failure was your fault?" I asked. She sat for several moments, apparently gaining control over her feelings, looked down at the floor and said, "In the twelve years that we were married we never once had intercourse. I know it was my fault; it was just that I was so afraid of penetration. I know that I should have gone to a doctor for help, but I was so embarrassed and we seemed to get along so well together that I never did."

Nancy went on to explain that it wasn't that she was frigid for they had had sexual times together which she had thought were satisfactory for both of them. Using manual stimulation, they each had achieved satisfaction in orgasm. She went on to say that she now knew it had not been a satisfactory relationship for her husband but that she wished he had said something to her or had suggested that she go to see a doctor. "He never once said anything," she stated.

I asked Nancy if she understood why her husband had not discussed the subject with her. When she indicated that she didn't, I went on to say, "Nancy, in most areas of life men are very willing to talk to their wives. However, in respect to their sexual relations with their wives, they are seldom willing to talk. If the sexual relationship is unsatisfactory, men usually feel that there is something very wrong with themselves. This is particularly true if the man has had no sexual relationship with other women to disprove this self-analysis. In other words, if men cannot help their wives to experience the same desires and satisfactions that they themselves experience, they are likely to feel that there is something wrong with themselves. A man's pride is very vulnerable in this area." Nancy accepted my interpretation saying that she had guessed that something like this must have been true in her case. Then she went on to say that after the breakup of their marriage she had gone completely to pieces and had undergone psychiatric treatment.

At the end of this first interview, I asked Nancy if she would mind if, as a matter of professional courtesy, I contacted her psychiatrist. I also stated that I thought he might be able to contribute information which would be of some help in our counseling sessions. She replied that she did not mind at all.

I called Nancy's psychiatrist and explained that Nancy had come to me for counseling but that I wanted to get his clearance and to hear his evaluation of Nancy's case. He replied that Nancy had first come to him in an extreme anxiety state. He had hospitalized her and placed her under sedation. He went on to say that he felt that Nancy could profit from counseling particularly since she had come voluntarily. He remarked that he felt the prognosis for Nancy was quite favorable and requested that I call him if any problems arose.

I asked the psychiatrist if he had come to any conclusions concerning Nancy's fear of penetration. He replied that he had talked over this problem rather thoroughly with Nancy and had concluded that it was not the result of any unresolved infantile problems. He went on to say that he believed this fear to be the result of a culturally determined attitude on Nancy's part combined with the naïveté of both spouses on their wedding night. That is to say, a painful first attempt at intercourse had fit in with Nancy's attitudinal set and had precluded any further successful attempts.

The Progress of Counseling

In the subsequent counseling sessions, Nancy's experience with her psychiatrist turned out to be a definite asset. She had learned to talk freely, and I could detect no reticence when she discussed intimate matters. As counseling continued, two major problems became apparent. First of all, Nancy was determined that she could have satisfactory sexual relationships and, secondly, that somehow she would get her husband back.

The first of these problems thoroughly taxed my permissiveness. For some six months, I listened to Nancy discuss the various men with whom she was having intercourse. She was cutting a swath across the community which included many individuals whom I knew. Her stories were confirmed by incidental anecdotal evidence from several sources.

I was not so concerned with the problem as a moral issue; but rather I was afraid that if her behavior continued it was bound to create an open scandal. This, I felt, would be exceedingly unfortunate for Nancy.

Nancy's promiscuity was combined with an extreme amount of drinking. Invariably her sexual relationships followed her drinking bouts. She reported that she pretended that her sexual partner was her husband. Nancy verbally recognized that her behavior was unacceptable, wrong, and dangerous. A frequent comment of her's was, "Dr.———, I know what I'm doing is wrong, but I can't help it." I could see nothing which would be accomplished by my attempting to intervene; nor could I see that criticising her behavior would help. Instead I decided to wait out the storm for I believed that if the situation did not blow up, time was in Nancy's favor. During this period I attempted to guide Nancy into considering why she was acting as she was and to accept the fact that she could not win her husband back by demonstrating her sexual prowess. Also, with some success, I attempted to get her interested in various community activities which were philanthropic in nature.

As might be expected, Nancy began to understand herself intellectually before she began to understand herself emotionally. I was encouraged to note that, as the counseling sessions continued, her drinking became more moderate in nature and her promiscuity was becoming more selective.

Counseling continued for another two months then Nancy felt that she no longer needed help. Her sexual excursions had decreased considerably. She was now limiting intercourse to single males for whom she had some respect and liking. Perhaps, even more importantly she had come to realize and accept the fact that she would not be able to win her husband back and that she would have to build a new life for herself. When Nancy left my office for the last time, it seemed to me that her expression of gratitude indicated that she had made great strides and that time would continue to heal the deep wound which had been opened.

Discussion

I do not take a great deal of credit for the successful outcome of this case. My decision not to intervene fortunately turned out well. I'll be the first to admit that there could have been disastrous results and that I continually felt that I was sitting on a community volcano. I believe that, as a result of her behavior, Nancy will undoubtedly have some guilt feelings; however, I think they will be much less than those which were excised by this very same behavior.

I would like to bring up two additional issues. Nancy's promiscuity could well have destroyed any number of marital relationships within the community. While I believe a counselor's first responsibility is to his client, what is his responsibility to the community? Should I have encouraged Nancy to be more selective? I personally knew some of the males who were involved. Should I have talked with them?

The second issue is with respect to marriage counseling in general. Nancy's problem is by no means limited to Nancy alone. Our culture's Victorian attitude toward sex continues to perpetuate marital adjustment problems which should not exist. It is an interesting but puzzling experience to find an intellectual recognition of a problem by the very individuals who have the problem and yet who have an emotional disability to do anything about it.

I am convinced that repression, in the Freudian sense, does not occur very frequently in this area today. I believe that the attitudes which exist, exist almost entirely on a consciously learned level. For the most part, they are learned in a negative way. It is that which is left unsaid and implied which is so destructive to sexual adjustment. The facts of procreation are taught quite well. However, the beauty of the sex act as the final expression of a united love is given minimal attention. Our attention is so consumed by the misuse and abuse of sex that we have quite forgotten that it can be a gift and, when properly given, the most precious gift that one person can give to another.

I have never quite understood why the misuse of sex should assume sinful proportions so out of line with any other type of unethical behavior. I do believe that our hysterical, emotional reactions to the abuse of sex are a major factor in keeping many individuals from ever experiencing the highest form of love in marriage. Dwelling on the "what might have been" keeps many a marriage from ever "becoming." Nancy should never have had to come to my office.

27...

Ethical Responsibilities of the Counselor in the Counseling Process

Counseling is, or is rapidly becoming, a profession. One of the marks of its professional status is an increasing and continuing concern with ethical problems. The old adage about an ounce of prevention being worth a pound of cure is particularly apropos in this area. Many of the ethical problems which arise in counseling could either have been avoided or settled with a minimum of concern if the counselor had considered them in advance or had been aware of his ethical responsibilities (Schwebel, 1955). It is the purpose of this chapter to set down some general guide lines and considerations for the practicing counselor.

The Legal Status of the Counselor

Wrenn (1952) has pointed out that the counselor actually has more legal protection, in a broad sense, than he may realize. A counselor does not have to release confidential information, personnel or counseling records, upon the *request* of a police officer, an officer of the court, or any other court official. Quite the contrary, the counselor should probably not release such information, for the counselee would then have every right to bring legal action against him. An exception to this statement may be found in those states, e.g., California, where the counselor may legally release information to certain public agencies and is protected under the law in the release of this information. However, in general, the only legal way in which a court can gain access to a counselor's records is by serving a warrant for the release of the records. Further, if the counselor keeps personal records which are not a part of the official records of the institution which he serves, these records do not have to be released when the official records are taken into custody.

The last comprehensive survey of the counselor's right to "privileged communication" was conducted by Smith (1956). At that time, Michigan was the only state in which the counselor was protected under the law. Gradually psychologists are getting certification in a number of states. This certification usually affords the psychologist the same rights for "privileged communication" as is given to ministers, lawyers, and physicians. In so far as councelors meet the requirements for certification they would, of course, have the same protection. However, for those counselors who are not certified the problem remains.

A California Attorney General's Opinion suggests that confidential communication, since it is information not required by law, *might be privileged*. While this is hardly a satisfactory state of affairs, it does suggest the possibility that in California, if the issue were to arise, counselors would have legal protection. Montana specifies privilege in civil proceedings only for any information obtained "in the study and observation of child mentality." Oklahoma makes it a misdemeanor for a teacher to reveal any information concerning a child, "except as may be required in the performance of his contractual duties." It would seem that Oklahoma counselors, if they are also considered teachers, should take a close look at their "contractual duties." Seven states empower the local board of education to rule on the disposition of information, as long as there is no legislation to the contrary. Thirty-seven states have no laws or rulings which are of any help to a counselor in the withholding of confidential information. The writer was unable to find any information, with respect to this problem, for the new states of Hawaii or Alaska.

Counselors should note that where they do not have privileged communication, they do not have an obligation to reveal confidential information unless they are under oath before a court of law. The mere request for the information, on the part of an officer or court official, does not obligate a counselor to reveal the information. If, under oath, a counselor refused to reveal confidential information, he could be cited for contempt of court. It would behoove counselors to be very certain that they are justified to withhold such information. It is likely that if the counselor's case for the withholding of such information were very strong, his professional societies, such as the American Psychological Association or the American Personnel and Guidance Association, would come to his aid. However, the counselor should make his decision to withhold legally requested information on the basis of his own personal and professional ethics and should not count on receiving aid from an outside source. It will take a number of favorable court decisions to establish precedent; and it is the writer's opinion that tests of a counselor's right to privileged communication should very clearly concern a violation of counseling ethics since unfavorable decisions will not strengthen the counseling profession's position (Carter, 1954).

Another point to consider is the possession of "hearsay evidence" (Wrenn, 1952). When a counselor possesses information that a counselee has broken a law and this information has been gained in a counseling session, it is likely to be considered as "hearsay evidence." This type of evidence is not generally admissable in a court of law. Certainly an objection by an attorney as to the admissibility of the evidence would, in most cases, rule out the information. As much of what is gained in a counseling interview is "hearsay evidence," the possession of such information will not normally be a legal problem although it may be an ethical problem for the counselor. Further, the possession of such information, while an ethical problem, is not a legal problem *until* the counselor is under oath. Many problems of this nature can be readily solved by encouraging the counselee to go to the proper authorities himself. The fact that a counselee reveals something of this nature to his counselor frequently indicates that he is asking for support and encouragement in making restitution.

In a juvenile court case, "hearsay evidence" may carry more weight. Attorneys are usually not present and the admissibility of evidence is left to the discretion of the judge. In an instance of this nature the counselor will have to decide for himself whether or not his testimony is a violation of counseling ethics and in the best interest of the counselee and society.

None of the foregoing should be interpreted to mean that the coun-

selor will not cooperate with an agent of soc[...]
has been said is only to point out that counse[...]
tection under the law than they realize and [...]
under an obligation to "reveal all" upon rec[...]
tion and discretion.

Ethical Principles in Counseling

Ethical standards which are of importance for counselors have been proposed from a number of sources (Gluck, 1952; Wrenn, 1952; Committee on Ethical Standards for Psychologists, 1953; Hahn and MacLean, 1955; Smith, 1956; Committee on the Preparation of Ethical Standards, 1959, 1961). Many of these standards are equally applicable to all of those who are in the helping professions. Some of the more pertinent of these standards will be rephrased and discussed with respect to the cases presented in this book.

Counselors, in all areas of work, should clearly recognize the limits of their competence and should not offer services which fail to meet the professional standards of recognized specialists in particular fields. Furthermore, a counselor should not attempt to diagnose, treat, or advise a counselee with reference to problems which are not within the counseling domain. A clear instance of this type of situation may be found in "A Case for Referral." Eddy was most definitely *not* a case for a school counselor. However, the counselor did have the responsibility to see that Eddy was properly referred and to be as helpful as possible in the process of referral. In the case called "Supportive Counseling," we have a situation where Karen was unable to receive the referral which was needed. The counselor attempted to get psychiatric aid for Karen but was unable to do so. Certainly this placed the counselor in a difficult position. The counselor recognized her limitations, however, and attempted to give Karen the understanding relationship needed; but she did not attempt to work outside of her area of competency. When, for some reason, a referral is impossible, a counselor will need to carefully weigh the pros and cons for continuing the relationship. The case entitled, "A One Man Wrecking Crew," is an example of a counselor who was insensitive to the needs of Mac and to his own limitations as a counselor. A referral should have been made long before it was initiated.

A counselor should not normally accept a counselee who is receiv-

chological assistance from another professional worker unless reement has been reached as to the respective areas of help being ered, or unless the counselee's former professional relationship has been terminated. This principle has both ethical and practical implications. Counselors, far more than they do at the present time, should work in cooperation with other agencies and professional workers (Mitchell, 1955; Shoben, 1955). Without this cooperation there can be much duplication of effort as well as a loss of valuable information. The establishment of a good inter-professional working relationship can be found in the case of, "No Desire to Live." This relationship turned out to be a very profitable one for Irene. In the case of "It Was a Happy Marriage," the counselor was not obligated to call Nancy's psychiatrist as the relationship had been terminated. However, the procedure he used was an excellent one to follow. He found out from the psychiatrist that Nancy's problem was within the counseling domain and was given some additional considerations which were helpful. If counselors wish to consider themselves as professional people, they will need to develop professional relationships.

The counselor should also insist on ethical standards with respect to his associates. In the case of "No Desire to Live," it will be remembered that the counselor sensitized the various school personnel to Irene's problem. This could have had disastrous effects, particularly if the counselor did not acquaint the school personnel with the need for maintaining this information in the strictest of confidence. As a general rule, the counselee's permission should be gained before communicating any information to another person or agency. This was done in the cases of " No Desire to Live" and "Nobody Understands Me." It was not done in "You're Supposed to Help Us." In this case the personal welfare of the counselee was at stake, and the counselor quite correctly placed this responsibility over the responsibility of maintaining a confidence.

A counselor in a school setting should assume, until proven wrong, that other school personnel are capable of maintaining confidences. He should be quite sure that they are aware of the need and the reasons for maintaining this confidence. If the counselor finds that his professional colleagues are not able to act in a professional manner, he should withhold confidences even though their knowledge of the counselee's problem might benefit the counselee. Many times a counselor can sensitize teachers to the fact that a child has a problem without being specific about what has been told the counselor in confidence. The welfare of the counselee is a primary consideration, and considerable thought should be given to this before a confidence is revealed (without the counselee's permission) to teachers or other professional people.

The counselor should guard confidences which are extended to him in respect to a counselee. When information is gained from other professional workers or parents, it is not wise in most instances to inform the counselee that the information has been obtained. This is not to say that the counselee should be unaware of the fact that the counselor has contacted and is working with the pertinent outside agencies (although it is desirable to get the counselee's permission to make this contact); but rather it indicates that by telling the counselee of the information obtained, the counselor may be destroying another very essential relationship. "They All Kick You When You're Down" illustrates this point. In this case the counselor reveals to the counselee that he has found out that she is making no attempt to find a job. This information was given to the counselor by Mary's social worker. It would be apparent to Mary that this was the only possible source for the counselor to have received the information. If the counselor wished to use this data, he could have questioned Mary in a directive fashion without ever revealing that he had the information. As a rule the only time a counselor should reveal a confidence received from another professional or, for that matter, a confidence received from a counselee, is when it is quite clear that there is imminent danger to the counselee or to society. If permission is given to release the confidence it, of course, ceases to be an ethical problem.

A counselor should present or report his findings, with respect to a counselee, accurately, simply, and in language which facilitates understanding. It should not be assumed that the referral source, or the recipient of the report, understands complicated psychological jargon unless this is known to be true. In many instances the counselor does not have the professional training to make a diagnostic judgement (e.g., schizophrenic behavior); and typing a counselee with such a term can have deleterious effects. If the counselor feels that the counselee has an emotional problem, he can state, "I feel that the counselee has an emotional problem." Psychological nomenclature which is misused, and even sometimes when correctly used, can be harmful. The rule is that any communication concerning a client should *promote* the welfare of the client. It should be insured that any recipient of a communication, concerning a counselee, can understand and profit from the communication. With respect to this, the professional training and experience of the recipient, if known, should be considered.

The counselor should refuse to suggest or support unwarranted assumptions, invalid applications, or unjustified conclusions with respect to psychological instruments or techniques. Psychological testing which is done under substandard conditions is not only invalid but unethical. Psychological instruments have been developed for specific purposes. An ethical principal may well be violated when these instruments are used for some other purpose. Consider the use of psychological testing in the case of "To Hell With My Mother" where Lewis was given aptitude and interest measures so that he could justify to himself his need for continuing counseling. The use of testing for this purpose is most questionable.

Counselors may also find that there is a tendency to generalize their conclusions beyond the supportive test evidence. This is frequently done with the individual intelligence tests when questionable clinical conclusions are drawn from very meager evidence. In the same vein of thought, many counselors have had an introductory course in the use of projective techniques. While this experience is valuable in sensitizing the counselor to an area of personality evaluation, the use of these same tests for diagnosis, without much more extensive training, is most unethical and may be harmful to the counselee.

A cardinal obligation of the counselor is to respect the integrity and protect the welfare of the counselee. A careful consideration of this principle should be maintained by the counselor at all times. A counselor's ultimate responsibility is to society, and his professional behavior should reflect his awareness of this. The welfare of the counseling profession and the welfare of the counselor are clearly subordinate to the welfare of society. In most instances the welfare of society can be best served by protecting the welfare of the counselee. Only when it is quite clear that either society or the counselee is in imminent danger should a counselor consider breaking a counseling confidence. In "It Was a Happy Marriage," the counselor raises the question of whether or not he should have sensitized Nancy's amours to the possible consequences of their relationships with Nancy. It would seem that the ethical answer to this question would be that the counselor should not have done so. These individuals were responsible for themselves as, in the final analysis, was Nancy. Granted that a potentially explosive situation existed, it was not a situation that falls under this principle. If, on the other hand, the counselor felt that Nancy had suicidal or homicidal tendencies, then he would have been obligated to take some action to either protect Nancy or society.

Counselors should not normally enter into counseling relationships with close friends or members of their own families. The experiences of many counselors suggest that the complications which arise out of a counseling relationship of this nature largely negate any positive gains.

As a counselor is a member of a profession which is primarily a helping profession, he should be willing to devote part of his services to work not included in his duties, or for which he will receive little, if any, financial return. Ellen in "What Shall I Do?" is a case in point. The counselor quite correctly aided Ellen although Ellen was no longer connected with the public school. Counselors will have requests for help where the counselee is unable to pay for the service. An additional comment should be made here; and that is the counselor should be very sure that the counselee cannot afford to pay at least a token fee if this is the customary practice. In our society a premium is placed on that for which we pay financially. Frequently, services which are offered for nothing are evaluated at the same level.

Bordin (1955), in a discussion of the counselor's ethical problems, notes that there are four areas of counselor responsibility to be considered in ethical decisions. The counselor has an ethical responsibility: to his society, to his sponsoring unit, to his client, and to his profession. It might be added that there is another source of ethical consideration; and that is the counselor himself. Most certainly a counselor's own values will enter into his ethical decisions. As it is impossible to state precisely what personal ethical standards a counselor should hold, particularly in a constantly shifting environment and society, about all that can be said is that a counselor should be aware of his values and his reasons for holding them. A counselor should not insist that all individuals hold the same standards that he personally holds. This is not to imply that a counselor must compromise his personal standards, but it should be remembered that they are *personal* standards. A statement from the *Ethical Standards of Psychologists* (Committee on Ethical Standards for Psychologists, 1953) is worthy of note as it applies equally well to counselors.

Very often the resolution of ethical problems requires that the psychologist choose between two or more interests that are in conflict. Are the psychologist's obligations primarily to the social group, or to his individual client, or to the profession, or to himself? There is, of course, no simple answer to this question. Most situations where ethical decisions are necessary involve an implicit hierarchy of values, and this hierarchy has to be redefined for each situation. The equation of ethical responsibility is a complex one: weights for the variables must be computed anew as each new ethical problem is solved.

How Do Counselors Feel About Ethical Problems?

A study by Smith (1956) will be considered in some detail because of its pertinence to this topic and because of the large number of counselors found in the secondary schools. In this study professional members of the National Vocational Guidance Association submitted critical incidents in which ethical decisions were involved. From these incidents an ethical questionnaire was constructed. This, in turn, was sent to 1,225 professional members of this same organization. Six hundred questionnaires, or approximately 50 per cent, were returned. The questionnaire was scored to indicate the degree to which the respondents would favor revealing confidential information to some authorized agency or person. A near normal distribution of scores was found. A high score on the questionnaire indicated that the respondent favored revealing confidential information to an authorized agency or person; a low score indicated the converse. In other words, a high score indicated that the respondent's major loyalty was to society; a low score indicated that the counselor's major loyalty, or feeling of responsibility, was to the counselee. The group which was the most closely associated with secondary school counseling showed the greatest preference for social obligation choices. Public school employees emphasized civil responsibility more than did any other occupational field. All educational counselors below the college level were significantly higher in social obligation choices than were college counselors. The greater the amount of public school teaching experience the respondent had, the greater was his degree of loyalty to society, and the lesser was his feeling of loyalty to the counselee.

One hopeful sign was found; and this was that the more graduate units in guidance, psychology, and related subjects, the greater was the loyalty of the respondent to the counselee. Respondents with the doctorate had the lowest mean scores on the questionnaire or were the highest counselee-centered group. Neither the amount of counseling experience nor the amount of time devoted to counseling proved to be a significant factor when comparing responses to the questionnaire.

A comparison of related items concerning access to cumulative records ranked administrators, other counselors, parents, teachers, social welfare agencies, law enforcement agencies, and employers, in decreasing order for accessibility to the records. Availability of records to the latter two groups was extremely debatable. The respondents tended to agree that personal problem information should not be available, but they tended to disagree as to whether administrators, other counselors, welfare agencies, or the counselee himself should have access to this information. Three fourths of the respondents agreed that when information was received directly from the counselee, the counselor had a responsibility to maintain the confidence.

Smith concludes that, with the exception of imminent harm to the counselee or others, respondents tended to place loyalty to the counselee above loyalty to society, although there was a tendency for public secondary school counselors not to share this direction of loyalty. Based upon the concurrence of at least 70 per cent of the respondents, Smith proposes that the following ethical standards be considered by counselors:

1. The counselee commands the primary loyalty of the counselor under ordinary conditions.

2. A counselor is justified in revealing confidential information to selected individuals when the counselee or others are in imminent physical danger.

3. A counselor should not voluntarily, nor upon request of the police, reveal counselee information of any offense short of guilt of a major crime.

4. A counselor should not voluntarily, nor upon request of administrators or parents, reveal any information about a counselee or former counselee received in confidence.

5. A counselor is not released from maintaining a confidence because others have the same knowledge.

6. A counselor is released from maintaining a confidence if he gains the counselee's consent to reveal such information.

7. When two counselees are seeking help on a mutual problem, a counselor should not reveal either counselee's confidence to the other.

8. When two counselors are working with the same counselee, it is ethical for them to share confidential information.

9. Confidential information may be revealed to another counselor if the counselee's anonymity is maintained.

Smith also proposes the following standards relating to the confidentiality of cumulative records:

1. Cumulative records should contain a counselee's transcript of grades, achievement test results, mental ability and other aptitude test results, interest inventories, personal problem information, and discipline records.

2. Teachers and other counselors who are directly concerned should have routine access to all cumulative record data except discipline and personal problem information.

3. All data concerning a counselee, except personal problem information, should be available to school administrators.

4. Parents and social welfare agencies should have access to achievement test results, interest inventories, and transcripts of grades.

5. A counselee should have access to his own transcript of grades and all test data except mental ability test results.

It might be said, as a practical criticism of these cumulative record proposals, that most schools have extremely lax filing systems. It is possible for almost any determined person to obtain access to cumulative record files with little difficulty. Furthermore, withholding materials from the files before handing them to a responsible person seems a little like questioning a person's patriotism. A more practical proposal might be for the counselor to keep a dual set of "books." In one set of files would be kept the materials on the student to which authorized personnel would have access. In the counselor's personal file would be kept the confidential materials on the counselee.

Lastly, Smith proposes several standards relating to other aspects of counseling:

1. A counselor should not intervene in a counselee's curriculum choice despite predictive evidence of academic or emotional outcomes.
2. A parent who has given information about a counselee's problem should be promised confidence.
3. A counselor's record of a counselee's psychotic behavior should be made available to other schools.
4. It is ethical for a counselor to gather information about a counselee from other schools without the counselee's consent.

It will be noted that almost all of Smith's proposals can be subsumed under the heading of counseling in a manner which will do the most to promote the counselee's welfare. It is also apparent from her study that there is a further need for school counselors to consider their ethical responsibilities in respect to their own school. Probably each school counselor should do this in conjunction with his administrator and the teaching personnel. Many of the ethical problems which arise in school counseling could be avoided if they had been considered before they arose. Counselors need to communicate their ethical responsibilities to those with whom they work.

Recording the Counseling Session

Tape recording a counseling session without the counselee's knowledge is an issue that is frequently raised under the heading of ethics. The opinion of this writer is that this is not an ethical problem. It is rather a question of wisdom. It is the counselor's responsibility to do that which is best for the welfare of the counselee. In almost all instances, it would be wise to obtain the counselee's permission to record a counseling session. Considering the effect it might have on the counselee if he discovers that the session has been recorded without his knowledge, the counselor should normally obtain his permission. However, there may be rare instances in which the counselor feels it is best for the counselee not to know that the session is being recorded. If the counselor is considering the welfare of the counselee in making this decision, it is not an unethical decision. Probably this issue has grown out of all porportion to what it deserves because of the use of counseling tapes for the training of counselors. The use of a counseling tape as an instructional aid, without the counselee's permission, is an unethical act. The counselee's permission should be obtained, preferably in writing, if the counseling tape is to be used for other than counseling purposes.

Conclusion

Schwebel (1955) believes that the causes of unethical behavior can be categorized into three areas: "The overpowering self-interest of the professional worker as expressed in personal profit, self-enhancement, and the maintenance of security and status; poor judgement, due in part at least to inexperience in problem solving in counseling; ignorance of technical knowledge and of one's own values." It may be that not much can be done to help the counselor in the first of Schwebel's categories. However, by being familiar with the problems which are likely to arise in the ethical area and by being adequately trained in counseling, the counselor should have little excuse for violations of ethical principles because of the last two categories.

Many of the considerations discussed in this chapter are common problems for counselors. The theme running through almost every ethical consideration raised is that the goals and purposes of society can be best served by keeping the welfare of the individual counselee as the paramount concern.

References

American Personnel and Guidance Association, Ethical Standards. *Personnel guid. J.,* 1961, *40,* 206–209.

Bordin, E. S. *Psychological Counseling.* New York: Appleton-Century-Crofts, Inc., 1955.

Carter, T. M. Professional immunity for guidance counselors. *Personnel guid. J.,* 1954, *33,* 130–135.

Committee on Ethical Standards for Psychologists. *Ethical Standards of Psychologists.* Washington, D.C.: The American Psychological Association, 1953.

Committee on the Preparation of Ethical Standards. A proposed code of ethics for A.P.G.A. *Personnel guid. J.,* 1959, *38,* 168–170.

Gluck, S. et al. A proposed code of ethics for counselors. *Occupations,* 1952, *30,* 484–490.

Hahn, M. E. and MacLean, M. S. *Counseling Psychology.* New York: McGraw-Hill Book Co., Inc., 1955.

Mitchell, H. E. A brief history of an interdisciplinary relationship. *J. couns. Psychol.,* 1955, *2,* 201–204.

Schwebel, M. Why? unethical practice. *J. couns. Psychol.*, 1955, 2, 122–128.

Shoben, E. J., Jr. Some thoughts on interprofessional relationships. *J. couns. Psychol.*, 1955, 2, 196–201.

Smith, Carol E. *Development of Ethical Standards in the Secondary School Counseling Relationship for the Use of Counseling Information.* Unpublished Doctoral Dissertation, University of Southern California, 1956.

Wrenn, C. G. The ethics of counseling. *Educ. psychol. Measmt.*, 1952, *12*, 161–177.

Index

163